Raising Toddlers

You Are Not a Bad Parent!
Practical Strategies for Parenting
and Disciplining Your Child

Lindsay Moore

Table of Contents

Introduction

I understand you. I have traveled the world with my family and am a lifelong health and wellness, food and crafts enthusiast. I am also a mother of two boys. I understand your joys, worries, and frustrations of raising a toddler. I know that you think you are alone, that you think you are a bad parent, but I assure you, you're not. You are a great parent. Everything your toddler is doing is normal. It is all a part of their development.

You are standing in the check-out aisle of your local grocery store when your toddler reaches for a candy bar. You tell them "no" to the candy bar, and suddenly, your child starts crying and begging. You quickly look around to see how many people are near you. You see the judgmental and sympathetic looks. In an effort to quiet your child, you offer them a smaller treat. You then notice another person giving you a judgmental look. It seems like no matter what you do, someone is going to be parent shaming you.

Parent shaming is a new phrase that has come to light since the growth of social media. Today, most parents feel like they are going to be judged, shamed, or feel like a bad parent because they are trying to raise their children the best way they know how. As a parent, you want what every parent wants for their child - for them to grow up into a happy and compassionate adult.

Raising a child is not an easy responsibility. It is the hardest job you will hold in your life. However, it is also the most rewarding, even during those difficult times when your child is asking for their fifth glass of water at bedtime or refusing to eat the food cooked at their request. While each age brings its own rewards and challenges, it seems that parents are more likely to be shamed when their children are toddlers.

Parent shaming is not just something other people do to us. We also shame ourselves. Parents will often lay in bed at night and think about the mistakes they made that day. They will tell themselves how they can be a better parent. They will wonder if they are good enough for their children. The biggest effect of parent shaming is it makes us believe we are bad parents.

The fact is, you are not a bad parent. You are an amazing parent who is doing their best for their children. Sure, we all have those moments when we feel like a bad parent. They come when our child is screaming in the parking lot. We feel like a bad parent when we can't give our children what they want. We even feel bad when we need to discipline our children.

It's important to remember that every child will grow at their own pace. Parents often feel if their child doesn't start crawling or walking by a certain age, something is wrong. While you always want to be honest with the doctor, there is nothing wrong with a child learning how to walk after a year or walking before they crawl.

There are a lot of parenting books out there that discuss developmental expectations. The authors will often discuss how they are experts in the developmental process of children because they hold degrees. While education is a great focus to have for a parenting book, this is not my focus. I am the mother of two boys, one now a preteen and the other a teen. Like you, I read parenting books written by experts to try to get a grasp on how to be the best parent. Like you, I had this ideal image of the type of mother I would be from the time I found out I was pregnant with my first child. I also learned that life doesn't always work the way experts want them to and this doesn't mean I am doing anything wrong.

This book isn't here to make you feel your child needs to be at a certain developmental level by 12 months or 2 years. This book gives you the most realistic developmental expectations. This information is taken from sources that discuss the average child's development. If your child takes a couple more months to reach a certain behavior or stage of development, don't worry. Your child is thriving just like all the other children in the world. The biggest factor to remember is that you are your child's biggest teacher. Learn about their developmental stages, so you can help guide them in the best ways possible.

CHAPTER 1:

12 Months to 18 Months

You baby just hit a milestone – they just celebrated their first birthday. They are officially 12 months or 1 year old. You look at your messy child who is eating a cupcake in the best way they can and think back over the last year. By now, your child has started to talk in their baby language, they have learned to crawl, and they might have even taken a couple of steps. As you save this mental image into your memory bank, you begin to wonder what the next six months are going to hold for your baby.

Developmental Expectations

There is so much I can say about the development of a child who just turned one. They are constantly learning, and this can be wonderful and frustrating for them – and you. Trust me, you are not alone when it comes to thinking, "Is my child on the right developmental track?" or, "Am I doing everything I can for my baby?" Then, there is always the frustrating moments of, "What am I doing wrong? Why isn't my child walking yet?" First, you aren't doing anything wrong. Your child is on the right track, you are doing everything possible, and you are doing a great job. Your child is going through the same developmental stages as every other child.

Separation Anxiety

One of the strongest behaviors for this age is separation anxiety. This can start earlier than 12 months of age. However, it will last well into the age of one. It's important for you to understand this is a normal part of your child's development. You didn't do anything to cause them to become anxious at you leaving. Here are a few tips to help your child work through any separation anxiety.

1. Don't try to sneak away or leave when they are not looking. This can make your child's anxiety worse as they never know when you are going to leave. You always want to give your child the chance to say "bye-bye" or give you a goodbye kiss and hug.

2. Establish a goodbye routine. You can do this by waving goodbye to your child or giving them a hug or a kiss. You could also create a goodbye routine through a handshake, a short dance, or anything else that works. Whatever this routine is, you need to be consistent. Even if you are in a hurry or dropping your toddler off at daycare, take time for the goodbye routine.

3. Have a regular caregiver. This might be a babysitter who comes to your house or a daycare provider. Your child is working on developing trust with you and their caregiver. Changing caregivers often can cause your child to become confused and nervous, which can prolong separation anxiety.

Even if your child is crying, follow the routine and leave. With two children, I understand how painful it is to walk away when your child is crying. Rest assured, they typically stop crying and start playing as soon as they can't see you.

Throwing Things

One-year-old children are professionals at throwing anything in their path. While this is behavior parents immediately want to end, your child isn't trying to do anything wrong or be destructive. Toddlers are very curious. For example, your child is wondering what will happen when they throw a plate of food on the floor. They aren't doing it to try to make you mad or cause you to lose your patience. Whether they are throwing toys, food, or their sippy cup, it's all out of curiosity.

Yes, your toddler is going to continue to throw anything no matter how many times you say "no" or get mad. Their brains are still developing, and they won't remember what happened when they threw their food on the floor a few days ago.

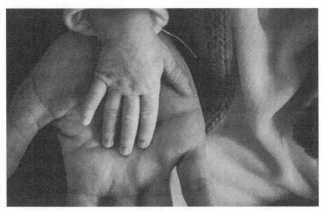

Self-Awareness

Near the end of this stage, you will start to notice your child struggling a little more when it comes to getting into their car seat, stroller, high chair, or taking a bath. This starts to happen because they are coming to realize they are a separate entity. Once they realize this, they will start to assert independence. This is a moment that is often bittersweet. You want to keep your child little for as long as possible, yet seeing them grow and develop is truly amazing. While you can't stop their independence, you can do your best to have patience and work with your child as they are trying to learn new skills.

Part of self-awareness is learning about themselves in a mirror. Let your child look at themselves through a mirror every day so they can observe their physical self and movements. You can also take this time to start building their self-confidence and playing with them. They will notice that you have your own movements and they have theirs.

Walking

Walking becomes a big milestone at this age. Not only will they start walking on their own, but they will start going up and downstairs. Once they start to trust their steps, you will find your toddler walking wherever they can. Of course, they are going to be a little off-balance from time to time. They will also start walking at a slower pace and then start to speed up. It's normal for your toddler to trip over their feet and lose their balance. While they are walking, it takes time to develop the coordination needed to maintain steps at a regular pace.

Climbing

Once they start walking, toddlers will start to climb onto everything they can, such as chairs, sofa, and beds. This also means that they will climb out of certain areas. For example, it is often around this stage where you will find your toddler climbing out of their crib, stroller, or high chair. One of the biggest worries for parents around this age is safety. While we all try to watch our toddlers every move, it is impossible. They are going to climb in and out of places, fall, and get hurt. Unfortunately, this is something that you can't always control. When your child does take a tumble, you need to remember that it's part of growing up.

Playing

At this age, toddlers become more active with their toys. They will start to push or pull toys, and dump toys out of a container; they might start to throw a ball (or other toys), and start to build objects. Your toddler is starting to learn how their toys work and why. This is the perfect age to give them toys where they have to match sizes and stack containers. Keeping your child active in play will help their intellectual development as well.

Introduce your toddler to crayons. Bigger sized crayons are the best because they will be easier to handle. They will spend their time drawing lines or scribbling. Give them a coloring book as your toddler will also be able to turn pages.

At this age, your toddler isn't going to play well with other children. Don't worry if you have a play date and find that your 12 to 18 months old are playing by themselves. This is normal. They need to learn to play by themselves before they can play with other children.

Language Development

Toddlers at this age have a very limited vocabulary. They will start to say a few words such as mama, dada, and kitty but nothing extensive. Some children might come close to saying their first sentence near the end of this developmental stage. Because their vocabulary is limited, it's important to remember that they don't understand a lot of words. As your child grows and develops, you always want to keep in mind that you need to talk to them in a way they will understand. For a child at this age, you want to keep communication as simple as possible. For example, if it's time for bed, you can say "night night." If it's time to eat, you can say "eat" or "food." You want to establish simple words they will be able to understand. Be consistent with the words you choose. Once they are able to understand that word, you can move on to build their vocabulary with another word that relates to the situation.

Some parents have started to teach their children sign language at this age. For example, they will teach their toddlers how to say "more" by using their hands. This is a great skill to start teaching your toddler. However, you want to keep it simple, just as you will with words.

The Noise!

If your world hasn't become loud already – it will. A big part of your child's development at this age is playing with the loudest toys they have and banging on pots and pans. I understand how annoying this can be at times, but trust me, it does end. All the loudness helps strengthen your child's intellectual abilities. Plus, it can often bring them happiness.

It's Their World

To your toddler, the world revolves around them. This is a normal part of growth and often called the "mine" or "me" stage. This is when they will grab things they want and not care who they are taking it from. However, if another child does start to cry, they do tend to pay attention to this reaction. While it is not always easy to teach your child not to grab objects from other people, it's important to let them see the reactions that occur. For example, if you are at a playdate and your toddler grabs a toy from another child, don't intervene until the child reacts. Your toddler will note this reaction and then you can find a simple way to explain grabbing toys from someone else isn't nice. Your child isn't going to understand this concept immediately, but over time, they will start to learn. Like any other developmental phase your child goes through, you need to go through it too.

Their intellectual development to understand the wants and needs of others is still growing. Right now, they are focused on what they need and want. This is a healthy process in development. Think about it this way – you cannot help anyone if you don't understand what you need. Your toddler is the same way. They need to understand themselves before they can understand someone else.

Learning Objects and Body Parts

This stage brings the perfect opportunity to play some fun educational games with your toddler. They are starting to learn the parts of their body, names for toys, food, and other objects in their world. For example, you can ask them questions like, "Where is your nose?" and they will be able to point to their nose. You can ask them to find a book and they will bring you a book or point to it.

What Can You Do to Support Your Child's Development?

We all want to do what is best for your children and supporting their developmental stages is highly important. Along with this comes the worry and wondering if you are doing everything you can. Believe me, I have stayed up late worrying about how I am doing as a parent. I will find myself going over the events of the day and wondering if I made the right decision or thinking about my mistakes. We all have these moments and the best thing we can do is take a couple of deep breaths and realize we are doing our best. Trust me, your children are not going to remember your mistakes. They are going to remember how you helped them, the love you gave them, the confidence, happiness, and how you tried your best.

Because I have been there, I want to extend some of my best advice to you during this stage of your child's development.

1. *Praise your child's process along with the result.* Parents often look at the end result and give their child praise. But when your child is learning, it's important to look at the bigger picture. Tell them how proud you are about every step they took. You want your children not just to feel good about the result, but also their efforts.

2. *Let them problem-solve.* I know how hard it is to see your child struggling in any way. However,

you will help them learn to develop their skills by allowing them to problem-solve. While you can help them through the process, ensure you do not take over. Let your child try their way and once you see them becoming frustrated, jump in and work with them. Then, once the problem has been solved, praise their efforts and the outcome.

3. *Reach into your inner child.* We all still have an inner child and one of the best ways to help our children grow is to think like them. Remember, everything is new to them at this stage. If your child is walking down the sidewalk and stops to pick up a rock, don't rush them. Allow them to feel and observe the rock. Observe their facial expressions as they are learning.

Feeding Themselves

Your toddler will start to feed themselves at this age. Because using a utensil will still be a bit challenging, they will use their hands. While this might not be the parents' ideal way for their toddler to eat, it's part of your child's development. Using their hands helps them gain coordination in bringing food from their hand into their mouth. They will start to use a spoon or fork in time.

Nutritional Needs

Your child is learning how to eat by themselves. They are eating solid foods and figuring out what foods they like and what food they don't. Sometimes parents struggle when it comes to their children refusing food. We get frustrated because we spent our time cooking, it's been a long day, we are tired, and so many other reasons. Don't worry about feeling this way because it is normal – for you and your child.

Your child doesn't know what foods they like or don't like. They are just learning about different food which we have eaten our whole lives. Plus, all children become picky eaters a time or two throughout their lives. It's part of development. It doesn't mean you don't know how to cook, or you aren't feeding your child what they like.

Whole Milk

One of the biggest transitions starting at this age is going to be switching your toddler to whole milk. Many parents fear the reactions their child is going to have. It's true, your toddler might not like whole milk. However, it is important for their growth and development. While you never want to force your child to drink whole milk, you can start introducing it slowly.

First, you can start by giving them half whole milk and mix it with your breast milk or formula. This will ease them into the milk. After a while, you can switch it to about ¾ whole milk and ¼ breast milk or formula.

Another way to introduce whole milk is to add a little water to it. Some parents will add ice cubes as this will not only give the milk a lighter taste for your child, but it will also keep it cold longer. However, you also want to ensure you don't water down the milk too much as they need the nutrients. Start with about ¾ milk and ¼ water or several ice cubes. From there you can decrease the ice cubes or go down to ⅛ water.

The best amount of milk to give them every day is about 16 to 24 ounces. While they need it for strong bones and development, giving them too much can interfere with other nutrients. You also need to remember their stomach is only about the size of their fist. Therefore, they will fill up on milk if given too much.

If your child does struggle with whole milk, here are some alternatives:

- ¾ cup of yogurt, cheese sticks or slices, ¼ cup of cottage cheese, and other foods with milk products.
- Continue with breast milk. Your child might not be ready to make the switch, and this is fine.

Introducing New Foods

You don't know how your child is going to react to new foods and this can be a scary moment for parents. You can find yourself making a meal after meal without your child eating much. Part of this is because they have much smaller stomachs than we do. Another reason is that the food is new to them. This will cause them to be hesitant and not try the food. If you start to feel your child isn't getting the nutrients they need, talk to their pediatrician.

As you introduce new foods, some of the best foods to start with are vegetables and fruits. Start with the ones you believe your child is going to like the best and then work in fruits and vegetables they might not care for. There are always going to be some food children won't eat. This could be because of texture, smell, or they don't see you eating the food. Children mimic your behavior and actions, which means if you eat when they do, they are more likely to eat.

Portions

When it comes to grains, your child should have about five to six servings of 100% whole grains a day. You can give them a slice of bread, One cup of whole grain cereal, or ½ cup of hot cereal.

Your child should have two to three servings of meat a day. If you are vegetarian or vegan, you will want to use alternatives — for example, one egg, three to six tablespoons of tofu, one tablespoon of peanut butter.

When it comes to vegetables and fruit, they should have five or more in a day. You should always try to get your child to eat one green vegetable servings in a day. Chop up the fruit or vegetable into small pieces and give them about a ½ cup, cooked or raw. If you mash the fruit or vegetables, you will want them to eat about two to four tablespoons.

At this point, giving your child finger foods is best. While they will learn how to use a spoon or fork, children are naturally more likely to use their fingers. It's always a good idea to steam or cook the harder fruits and vegetables, such as apples and cauliflower. You also want to ensure the pieces are small enough for your child. Even berries should be cut in half.

Healthy Snacks

Some of the healthiest snacks to give your toddler are fruits and vegetables. If you want to introduce your toddler to carrots, you will want to shred and cut the carrot. Sometimes when you shred the carrot into pieces, they can be a bit long, which can cause a one-year-old to choke.

Other healthy snack ideas include:

- applesauce
- one scrambled egg
- string cheese, which you will want to chop
- a ¼ to ½ cup of mashed potatoes mixed with chopped broccoli or another vegetable

Parenting Tips for Difficult Moments

Tantrums and Meltdowns

There is no control when it comes to your toddler's emotions. They also don't understand their emotions, which can cause them to feel confused. At the same time, they have trouble expressing their emotions because their vocabulary is so limited. This is why they will often have temper tantrums or meltdowns. It's one of the few ways they can express their emotions.

The dreaded tantrums. They always seem to happen when you are in a public location. They seem to happen at the worst possible moment. Sometimes you know when your child is about to have a meltdown and other times, they will catch you off guard. Every parent will tell you that some of the most difficult moments with their children are when they are throwing a temper tantrum. The biggest reason for this is because parents struggle to know what to do when their toddler has a tantrum.

Some parents will tell you the best step to take when your child is having a meltdown is to ignore them. But, before you follow this advice, take a moment to think about how your child feels. The main reason why toddlers at this age throw a tantrum is that they don't understand. They only understand a few words and most parents don't explain something to their child in a way they can understand. Therefore, your toddler becomes confused, frustrated, and reacts in the best way they know how – by having a tantrum.

At this stage, handling a tantrum is still a bit easy because they are easily distracted. You can use anything they can play with or watch. For example, if you are heading out to run a few errands, bring a couple of your child's toys with you. If you notice a tantrum is about to begin, bring one of the toys out and act excited. Most of the time, this will distract your toddler from what was about to cause the tantrum.

It is important to remember that sometimes nothing will stop your child from having a meltdown. The emotions they feel might be too overwhelming, and having a meltdown is the only step they are able to take. Your child might be tired, having a bad day, or upset for another reason. Take time to comfort your child. We all want to quiet them down as quickly as possible because we are embarrassed or anxious about what other people are thinking. However, the most important factor is that you need to take care of your child. You need to ensure that they realize you acknowledge their emotions and are there for them. The comfort you can provide your child in their moment of need is more important than feeling embarrassed because your child is crying in the restaurant.

Sleeping

In total, your child should get about 14-15 hours of sleep in a 24-hour period. This includes about 11-12 hours every night and two naps during the day. Most parents will lay their one-year-old down in the late morning and then again in the afternoon. No matter when you decide to lay your child down for bedtime or their naps, you need to remain as consistent as possible. Consistency is going to decrease any type of sleeping problems that can arise during this age.

It's important to note that your children are going to wake up at least once during the night. They will often be alert and ready to play. You can decrease the chance of them waking up during the night by giving them a healthy snack before bed. At this age, children usually wake up during the night because they are hungry.

There will be days for every child where they don't want to nap, or they don't sleep well during the night. When these times arise, it's best to remain calm and do what you can to get your overstimulated child to sleep. Fortunately, there are a number of tips that you can follow to help ensure your child sleeps well.

1. *Give your child a few choices.* When your child becomes more independent, they will start to fight sleep and bedtime because it is too structured. They will start to feel like they don't have any control over the situation. Your child is like you; they want to feel in control. Therefore, you can give your child choices, such as what pajamas to wear or what book to read. Don't give them too many choices as this can cause them to become overwhelmed. Instead, pick out a couple pairs of pajamas and a couple of books to choose from.

2. *Make the environment comfortable and calming.* It is natural for your children to have nightmares at this age. In order to decrease this sleeping problem, you want to try to create a peaceful environment in their room. Make sure your child feels safe with a night light, their favorite blanket, stuffed animal, or anything else. You can also play soft music to help them fall asleep.

3. *Don't allow your child to become overstimulated in the evening.* Like you, your child can feel stressed throughout the busy day. When your toddler starts to feel this way, it is hard for them to sleep because they are overstimulated. Do your best to ensure the couple of hours before their bedtime routine starts are calm and relaxing for them. Let them play quietly

before and after the evening meal. Don't play games which will cause them to get excited and run around. Give them a bath before their bedtime routine starts and maintain a soothing voice throughout the evening.

Mealtime

One day your child is going to eat well and the next day they will eat hardly anything. This causes most parents to worry about their child becoming sick. However, this is normal behavior for a one-year-old. Toddlers will eat when they are hungry. If they aren't hungry, they won't eat. Don't force your child to eat if they aren't hungry. You will notice if they are becoming sick and need to go to the doctor. If they aren't eating but are still your energetic and happy child, there is no need to worry.

Does your child only eat certain foods or the same thing for days in a row? This is also normal behavior. Part of the reason for this is because children at this age love routine. It helps them feel safe. Another reason is that they will go through phases. They are enjoying the food. Continue to give them food but ensure they are also getting the other food groups, at least as much as possible.

Noncompliance

Discipline can be difficult for a 12 to 18-month-old because of their limited understanding. The key is to remain consistent with the discipline and they will start to understand certain behaviors are wrong. Always remember, discipline is not about punishing; it's about guiding the child, so they learn the difference between right and wrong.

Your child has a good set of lungs and they enjoy using them everywhere they go. While it is fine for them to test their vocal cords at home, it isn't appropriate in church or other places. Therefore, you need to start to teach them when and where they can use their loud voices and when they need their quiet voice. At that age, one of the best steps to take is to introduce a quiet voice. This will take time, but your child will catch on faster than you know it. You can use the word "quiet" or you can establish your own expression.

Some parents want to stop their child from whining. One of the best ways to do this is to treat it like a meltdown – distract them. You can try using a toy or create a game to get them to laugh and lift their mood.

Sleep and Napping Guidance

Establishing Routines

At this age, your toddler can't handle a lot of unpredictable moments. This is because they expect things to follow a routine and want to know what is going to happen next. It's important to do what you can to stay in the routine as it will limit the feeling of stress. When your child is stressed, they will often become irritable and fussy.

This is around the age where you should start a bedtime routine with your toddler. With a routine, your child will be able to understand when bedtime is coming, what they do before they go to bed, and when it's time to lay down and go to sleep. At this age, children don't understand time. Furthermore, their mind and memory are still developing. This means that they need to have a routine, so they don't become surprised when it's time for bed or a nap.

Have you ever noticed how easily children can become distracted or discouraged when they have to do something, such as going to bed? They struggle because they don't understand that their bedtime is 7:30 P.M. This causes them to become confused, which is often the cause of a toddler's meltdown. By establishing a consistent bedtime routine, your toddler will go to bed with more ease.

One of the most important tips, when you establish a bedtime routine, is that you want to be consistent. You want to do the same routine every night. This means that the routine needs to work for your toddler, yourself, and other members of your family. Finding the best routine can be a challenge. You might find yourself switching the routine over the first few weeks. Fortunately, this won't cause too much stress on your toddler, especially if you establish the bedtime routine slowly.

Another important tip when establishing a routine is to let your toddler guide you. They will let you know what works for them and what doesn't through their actions. For example, if you start the routine with a bath and find your toddler running away from their room once they get out of the tub, you will want to think about readjusting this part of their bedtime routine. You can do this by giving them something to look forward to after their bath. This might mean that you and your child have a special playtime, or you place a sensory bin by their bedroom door that they can play in between their bath time and when they head to their bedroom.

Some parents like to create pictures and hang on their child's wall to help them understand their bedtime routine. For example, if the bedtime routine starts with reading a book, you will have an image of a book or a picture of you reading a book to your toddler. With each new step in the bedtime routine, ask your toddler to point to what they are going to do next.

A bedtime routine shouldn't take longer than 15 to 20 minutes. You want to ensure that you have a beginning and an end, so your child understands when it's time to start and go to sleep.

An example bedtime routine might look as follows:
- Picking a short book to read. At this age, board books are the best.
- Singing a lullaby
- Goodnight hug
- Laying down and being tucked in
- Goodnight kiss

Your Child's Biological Clock

People are born with a biological clock. This is the part of us that will wake us up at a certain time. You know you have a biological clock, and so does your child. A 12 to 18-month-old will sleep about 11 to 13 hours a day, including their nap. However, it doesn't always matter what time your child goes to sleep. They will still wake up and get their day started at the same time. Unfortunately, letting your child stay up past their bedtime is not going to allow them or you to sleep in. The only thing this is going to do is cause your child to have a hard day as they will most likely be crabby and tired.

CHAPTER 2:

18 Months to 2-Years-Old

Your child continues to grow before your eyes. You continue to be amazed by their developing personality, even as you are entering the terrible twos. The first factor to remember about entering the two-year mark is the "terrible twos" can start before they are 2-year-old. They can also start after they are two. The second factor to remember is that your child doesn't mean to anger or frustrate you. They are trying to learn, develop their personality, and understand life in general.

Realistic Developmental Expectations

Turn on the Music and Dance Away!

Engaging with your toddler is important. It can be easy to fall into the trap of telling them to stay out of things or to do something a different way when you are teaching them. Your days can often become frustrating and long with the amount of noise coming from them. Your patience will wear thin. It's okay to feel this way as it is part of being a parent. No matter how hard we try, the moments with our children won't always be fun and games. However, we can start to erase the stress for at least a few minutes or by turning up the music.

One of the greatest joys of this age is they start to dance. They might just bop up and down or from side to side, but they are having fun with the music. Join in and dance with your child.

Stop Putting Objects in Their Mouth

I have stated before all your child's phases are temporary. During this age, your child is going to start to move out of the sensory learning phase. They won't put everything they touch into their mouth. Of course, this doesn't mean they won't do it now and then. If they are naturally curious, they might put something in their mouth.

Starting to Understand Wrong from Right

You will start to notice your child is listening to some of your demands, they have stopped playing with the wall outlets, or doing other actions you've told them not to. This is because your child is starting to understand right from wrong and they are starting to realize if they do something you will get mad. They understand the concept of time-out and how it means they have done something wrong. They don't want to disobey you, even though there are moments it seems like they do.

For example, you hand your child a toy from the couch and tell them, "Clean this up." You know they understand you because this is your routine when they are helping you clean up at the end of the day. However, instead of putting the toy away, your child runs off and giggles. You start to feel they have completely ignored your request, but they haven't. First, your child might be aware that it's not clean up time because it's not the end of the day. Second, your child might have noticed something that was more interesting and got distracted.

Undress Themselves

While they might still need help, your child is well on their way to undressing themselves. They might even start to undress themselves the moment you mention it's bath time. They will also undress throughout the day. There will be times your child runs up to you with no clothes on. They have just hit a new milestone and they are excited about it. They will also start taking off their clothes whenever they feel like it. This can become a battle, especially if you are out in public. Your child doesn't understand you have to wear clothing in public. However, they might also be a bit warm if they start to take off clothes. Pay attention to their body temperature if it is hot and humid. It's better to let your child run around in a diaper than become overheated.

They Develop Shyness

Has your toddler suddenly started to become shy in front of people? If they have, this is a normal stage of development. Children can go from saying hi to strangers in the grocery store to hiding behind you. It's not something to worry about as toddlers will develop a stage of shyness. As your toddler grows, they start to understand and see social situations in a different way. They will become more cautious around strangers.

Expressing What They Like and Don't Like

Your toddler had a favorite yellow shirt that they wanted to wear whenever they could. One morning ask your toddler if they want to wear their favorite yellow shirt and they will respond with "No, don't like it." This can come as a shock to you as you don't understand how they loved this shirt a few days ago and now they don't want it. The bottom line for these types of changes is they are developing into their own person. Be happy your toddler is starting to show more of their personality. The more they are allowed to express their likes and dislikes at home, the more comfortable they will be.

Other Expectations

- Your child will begin talking about themselves. They love to tell and show you all the new skills they have. Pay attention and become as excited as they are. While we have known how to jump for years, they just learned. It is an exciting time!

- They will start to answer simple questions. Do they like the color green? Ask them and they will tell you.

- One of the best ways to get your child to learn is through interactive games. Play with them often. However, you should also remember it's important for your toddler to have their alone time as well.

- Yes, your toddler wants your attention – all the time. They are also at an age where you can start teaching them manners, such as why interrupting is wrong. But you also want to remember that children live in the moment. What they want to tell you now, they can quickly forget in a minute.

- Your toddler now understands when a toy disappears, it still exists.

Nutritional Needs

Meals

Your child should be eating about the same amount of servings at this stage as they did for the previous stage. The biggest factor is to pay more attention to their milk and iron consumption once they hit the 18-month mark. Children at this age can become iron deficient, which will affect their mental, behavioral, and physical development. Make sure your child is eating foods that are rich in iron at least three to four times a week. You also want to limit their milk consumption to 16 ounces.

Around 18 months is when you will start focusing more on iron-rich foods, such as beef, fish, and beans. Up until this age, you mainly gave your child cereal that was rich in iron. This cereal is now gone, which means you need to transition your child to food rich in iron.

Because a lack of iron can cause health conditions like anemia, it is best to talk to your child's health care provider about their iron consumption. You also want to note if they choose to drink a lot of milk as this can interfere with their iron.

Don't worry if your toddler skips meals every now and then. Sometimes they aren't very hungry and become more focused on a couple of healthy snacks throughout the day. They will eat when they are hungry.

Here are a couple of examples of balanced meals for your 18-month-old to 2-year-old:

Meal Plan for a Day

Breakfast: Berries with a whole-grain waffle

Morning snack: Cottage cheese and fruit

Lunch: Turkey on a whole grain tortilla with lettuce, tomato, and dressing.

Afternoon snack: Banana and apple slices

Supper: Fish with potatoes and green beans

Meal Plan for a Day

Breakfast: Super green mini muffins. This is a yogurt recipe. To make these, you will need the following ingredients:

- One egg
- One banana
- One-half cup of applesauce
- One-half teaspoon of baking soda
- Three-fourths cup of white flour
- Three-fourths cup of whole wheat flour
- One cup of plain yogurt
- Two cups of spinach

To make super green mini muffins:

1. Preheat your oven to 350 degrees
2. Spray the muffin tin
3. Mix the dry ingredients in a medium bowl

4. Combine the banana, yogurt, and spinach in a separate bowl

5. Add the applesauce and eggs into the dry ingredients and mix well

6. Add in the yogurt mixture to the medium bowl

7. Fill the muffin tins about ¾ full

8. Bake in the oven for 15 to 20 minutes

9. Serve with your choice of berries in the morning

Morning snack: Your child's favorite fruit or vegetable

Lunch: Light tuna on whole-grain toast with a vegetable

Afternoon snack: Banana and apple slices

Supper: Lasagna

Healthy Snacks

Fruit and yogurt pops are often a favorite healthy snack when it comes to your toddlers. This is also a way they can get their dairy in a fun way, especially during the summer.

What you will need to make fruit and yogurt pops:

- One cup of plain yogurt
- One cup of frozen or fresh fruit
- Four to six popsicle molds

The directions to make this recipe are as follows:

1. Blend the yogurt and fruit in a food processor until it is a smooth texture

2. Pour mixture into each popsicle mold until it is about ¾ full

3. Place the top on each mold and put into the freezer

4. Remove the molds from the freezer once the popsicles are solid and enjoy

A fruit and yogurt smoothie is another fun snack idea to give your child their daily nutrients. This is a great snack for the picky eaters.

The ingredients you will need to make this smoothie are:

- One-fourth cup of plain yogurt
- One-fourth cup for your choice of chopped fruit

The directions to make this recipe are as follows:

1. Mix the ingredients in a blender until they are smooth

2. Enjoy!

Parenting Tips for Difficult Moments

Tantrums and Meltdowns

Tantrums are going to become more common around this age. They will also build into hitting, kicking, and biting. Their emotions are continuing to develop, but they still struggle to explain how they feel. This is the main reason why they throw tantrums. Even if your child is crying at the top of their lungs because you don't have an apple for them to eat, it is because they don't understand.

Your child doesn't understand that situations change from one day to the next. For example, if they had an apple for a snack the previous day, they should be able to have one the next day. In their mind, you are able to take an apple out of the fridge because you have before. Therefore, when you tell them, "We don't have apples, would you like an orange?" they are going to become confused. When situations like this happen, you can use distractions to help your child through their confusion. However, you also want to acknowledge the way they feel. If you know your child loves oranges, continue to prepare the orange and offer it to them. You can even eat a piece and talk about how good it is. If your child is hungry enough, they will choose the orange.

Other than distractions, you also want to remain positive and calm during a tantrum. I understand this can be easier to say that do. However, it will help you and your child immensely if you remain calm. After all, your child knows when you are upset, which is going to make them upset. When you are calm, they will be able to calm down easier. There will be times where you will find remaining calm easier than other times. If you do lose your cool, don't feel guilty about it as it happens. Just try to use a technique to help you remain calm next time. Some of the best techniques are taking a few deep and slow breaths. You can also tell yourself, "It's okay. My child is frustrated. I can help them through this", or any other positive comments that will help you remain calm and focus.

There are always those moments when we want to discipline our children for temper tantrums. We don't want them to act that way in the store, so we want to set them in a time-out. Do your best not to discipline your child when they are having a temper tantrum. They are confused, frustrated, or angry because something isn't working for them or they don't understand. Do your best to keep this in mind, but don't worry if you lose your temper and place them in a time-out. This happens to parents all the time. We become frustrated over our child's frustrations. Be kind and gentle with yourself, just like you want to be with your child.

Sleeping

One of the biggest sleep milestones of this age is switching from a crib to a toddler bed. This is often an exciting yet frustrating time for parents. You want to do your best to understand your child is adjusting to their new bed. Yet, like any human, you also want to sleep. The fact is, this is one of those times where both you and your child can lose sleep for a few nights. Do whatever you can to remain calm and understanding of your child as they learn to trust their new bed.

Co-sleeping might be a thought you have when it comes to switching your child's bed. While you can sleep in your child's room, you don't want to do this for a very long time. Start by laying down next to their bed with your hand on their bed. This will assure them that you are there as they are falling asleep. Once they start to fall asleep, back away from their bed, don't back away too much, you want to watch your child's reaction to you moving from beside their bed. If they start to become stressed, move a little closer. If they are fine, stay in that spot for a while. As they continue to drift off, you can continue to back out of their bedroom. Soon, you will be in your own bed. This doesn't mean your child won't wake up during the night crying. However, it does give your child the added security that you are helping them through this transition.

Another way to co-sleep is to stay near the bed for a couple of nights. You will sleep there, which means it might help to have an air mattress for comfort. After a couple of nights, back away from their bed a bit and sleep in that spot for a couple of nights. You will continue to do this until you are by their door sleeping. After a week or two, they will be more comfortable sleeping in their bed, and you can move back to your bed.

Because you have moved them to a toddler bed, they are free to get up when they want. Your child will get up several times after you put them to bed. They will ask for more glasses of water than you can imagine. They will find any excuse they can come up with to get out of bed. The best way to handle this is to acknowledge their excuses, especially if they are emotional, and bring them back to bed. You might repeat this for an hour or two, but they will start to get up less. The key is to remain consistent and tell them that it is time for bed. Take time to tuck them in and give them a goodnight kiss or hug each time they get out of bed. Yes, this is going to be frustrating and you will find yourself begging the universe, your angels, or God to get your child to sleep. We all like our alone time for relaxation after our children go to bed. Remember, this is temporary. Before you know it, they will be going to bed and staying in their room.

Mealtime

This is around the age where you will start to have power struggles during meals. This is all part of your child's need to gain independence. It is frustrating and you will become angry from time to time. As you work on acknowledging your child's emotions, you also need to acknowledge yours. It's okay to feel negative about a situation. You are human and you can't always remain positive, no matter how hard you try. The key is to do your best and tell yourself you are doing your best. This is normal behavior from your child, and you are a great parent. Be proud of yourself as you are raising an independent child who is going to reach their dreams.

Toddlers are picky eaters. Your child, who used to eat easier or a variety of food, is now refusing to eat more food. They continue to want certain foods and you are unsure if they are getting their necessary servings. There is very little to worry about when it comes to your child and getting the right amount of nutrition for two reasons. First, when our bodies are missing a certain food group, we are more likely to crave this food. Listen to what your child wants to eat. If they are asking for chicken for a snack, their body is telling them they need protein. Let them have some chicken as a snack. Second, there are other ways to ensure your child is getting their nutrition through gummy vitamins and nutritional drinks or shakes. Talk to your child's pediatrician about some of the best choices for your toddler.

Another way to help your child through their picky stage is to offer choices. Put the macaroni and cheese, chicken, apple slices, and carrots on their plate as their choices. They will eat what they want and then you can save the rest for next time. You will be amazed what your child will eat when they are given choices.

If your toddler starts refusing to eat a certain food they used to love, such as green beans, stop serving them for a while. Focus on different foods and then bring this food back in a few weeks.

Do your best to stay away from junk food or limit it. The less junk food you bring into the house, the less your child is going to want to eat that food. If you want your child to focus on healthy eating, everyone needs to eat that way. Of course, you are going to hide certain foods to eat during your child's naptime. But, if you don't want your child to eat the food, don't eat it in front of your child. Trust me, when it comes to toddlers, they are going to want what is on your plate more than theirs. Keep the food the same.

Noncompliance

It is during this age that you are going to notice your child becoming more rebellious. One reason for this is because they are trying to gain independence. Another reason is that they become more open about their struggles to explain their emotions. The only way they know how to show you they are frustrated is through what you might consider their defiant behavior, such as temper tantrums, hitting, and biting.

There are several tips to help you deal with any type of noncompliance. First, you want to understand why your child is acting a certain way. You are at home and hear your child start crying in the next room. You walk into the room and see your child look up at a toy on the table. They are trying to reach it. You walk closer and ask, "Why are you crying?" Your child looks back at you and points to their toy on the table as they continue to reach for it. You then state, "Are you trying to get your toy? Let's get that down for you." It's important to explain your child's feelings to them. This tells them that you know what they are feeling and explains it so they can continue to learn. It also shows them that you will help them but gives them the chance to problem-solve and remain a little independent.

It's easy just to grab the toy your child wants and hand it to them. However, this can also make them more frustrated because they want to get it themselves. Think of ways that you can work with your child so they can grab the toy. For instance, you can give your child a little stool and help them step up or lift your child up to reach the toy. You can also push the toy to the part of the table where they can reach it themselves.

Hitting and biting are behaviors that can often make you immediately angry. It's important to remember that you want to discipline your child in a calm manner. Remember, aggression occurs because they are frustrated. If your child hits or bites another person, remove them from the environment right away and tell them, "No hitting, not nice." You can also tell your child it hurts the other person. Use words or phrases they understand and remain consistent.

It's important to always understand why non-compliant behavior is occurring. When your child hits or bites, think about what was going on during that time. What caused them to react in that way? Ask yourself if your child does this during a certain time of the day as they could be tired if it's close to their naptime or bedtime. How is your child acting when they hit or bite? Is it purely out of frustration or is something else going on at the same time? When you are able to get to the bottom of the behavior, you will be able to put a stop to it easily.

Another tip is to distract your child when they start to act out in a rebellious way. For example, your child wants to buckle themselves in their car seats. Let them try to do it themselves, especially when it is the first time. Of course, they are going to become frustrated because let's face it, even adults can struggle to buckle children up in a car seat. One way to distract them is by helping them buckle up through a saying or a song. As you help your child buckle up, you can sing, "And this is the way we buckle up, buckle up, buckle up. We are now buckled up and ready to go. Yay!"

During this age, your child should start picking up their own toys. With this task will come their refusal to do so. One of the best ways to handle cleaning up is to make it a game. If you've ever watched the television show, *Barney,* they created a catchy cleanup song. It goes "Clean up everybody, everywhere. Clean up, clean up, everybody do your share" (Barney - Clean Up Lyrics, n.d.). This is a simple tune that your child can understand. If there is another television show your child enjoys that has a cleanup routine, follow that. You can also create a routine with your child.

Sleep and Napping Guidance

Establishing Routines

By now, you should have some type of sleeping routine down. Of course, you will need to adjust your routine as your child becomes older. You might find yourself needing to adjust around the time they start becoming more independent. Another big step when an adjustment might be needed is when you switch from a crib to a toddler bed.

You will also have the adjustment of your child going down for only one nap throughout the day. While they will still sleep close to 11 hours a night, and might still wake up during the night, the best time for them to nap is in the early afternoon. Many parents like to put their child down a little after dinner. You want to ensure that they have had some time to walk around and play, as placing them down immediately after they eat can cause stomach issues. The child should sleep no longer than two to three hours during the day.

As you ease them into a different nap schedule, you will want to give them time to relax before their nap. You will also want to set a time, for instance, from 11:45 to 1:45. If your child is not up by the end of their scheduled time, wake them up slowly and gently. You don't want them to sleep too long because this will keep them from falling asleep during their regular bedtime.

Another tip when introducing them to a new naptime schedule is to lay them down a bit earlier in the first couple of weeks. It will take them a bit to adjust and fall asleep. Laying them down earlier will give them their needed rest.

Your Child's Biological Clock

Your child's biological clock is going to adjust to changes in their sleeping routine. Their bodies will naturally start to work on the right amount of sleep they need. Once your child is used to one nap throughout the day, they will start to get a bit tired before their naptime and wake up around the same time. The same goes for any changes in their nighttime schedule. Your child's biological clock is going to change when you help them change the schedule or on their own.

CHAPTER 3:

2 to 3-Years-Old

At the age of two, your child is pushing your buttons and starting to carry on short conversations with you. While you continue to be amazed by your child, you will go through a lot of emotions in one day. All the emotional roller coasters are natural. They are to be expected. There is nothing wrong with what you are feeling – even those moments where you wish you could have some time alone. Don't worry, I have been there too. You're not alone in this wish or thinking.

Realistic Developmental Expectations

Welcome to Pretend Play

Your toddler is going to spend more time in their imagination at this age. They might create a whole pretend world or a pretend friend and start talking to the air. Let your child engage in their pretend play, as this will help them develop the necessary skills to play with other children. Sometimes they will engage you in their pretend play. When they do this, have fun and play with them. It doesn't matter how silly you might look as you are taking care of your toddler's developmental needs. So, when your toddler hands you a pretend phone and tells you to talk to their friend, create a conversation and follow your toddler's guidance. For instance, your toddler might say, "Tell Tommy we meet at 6:00 to eat," so you tell Tommy this over the phone. When you are done talking to Tommy, your toddler will grab the phone and be on their way.

They will Become More Social

If you take your two-year-old to the park, they will start to play with another child, even if they have never met them before. Get to know the other child's parent and allow your children to play. Two-year-olds will go back and forth from playing with their new friends to playing by themselves. This is a normal developmental process. It doesn't mean that is uninterested in playing with the other children or something that happened they didn't like. The skills they need to learn when it comes to team playing takes time to build.

They are Better with Physical Balance... and Get Hurt

"Mommy, look what I can do!" I heard my son exclaim as he balanced on one foot. At this age, your child will become better with your physical balance. They will be able to run, jump, hop on one foot, and become an acrobat. Unfortunately, there will also be times they get hurt. No matter how hard we try to protect our children from getting hurt in the tumbling play, it is going to happen. When it does, there will be times you will feel guilty you didn't stop them and other times you will have the "I told you not to do that several times" thought. Acknowledge your emotions and thoughts as you comfort your child. There is no need to go through a lecture about how they shouldn't do this or that, they want your hugs and kisses to make their boo-boos better. They are learning what can hurt them naturally, which is sometimes the best way for children to learn.

Brushing Their Hair and Teeth

They might still need a little help at first, but they will quickly catch on to brushing their teeth and hair. At the same time, they will learn the importance of washing their hands and can start to learn how to wash their body in the bathtub. They will still struggle with grasping items, especially objects like crayons.

Do what you can to help your child grow with grasping and personal hygiene.

Memory Improvement

They will start to talk about past events in their own way. They will tell you what happened the other day or what they remember someone doing. Listen to their stories, even if you were there and remember the event. You will notice your child tells what happened in a different way. For instance, they might say, "When I was at Bev's house, the puppy ran around a lot and then went flying all around!" Of course, the puppy did not fly. Your child is using their imagination to enhance the story. There is no need to tell them "No, that's not how it happened" or "That's not really true" because your child doesn't understand truth and lies yet. Allow their imagination to expand as much as possible. They will start to learn the difference between truth and lies within the next few years.

Mother Goose and Nursery Rhymes

"The itsy-bitsy spider climbed up the waterspout. Down came the rain and washed the spider out. Out came the sun and dried up all the rain. And the itsy-bitsy spider climbed up the spout again" (Lullaby lyrics: Itsy-Bitsy Spider, 2018).

The Itsy Bitsy Spider is one of the most popular nursery songs that children love. Your child is now at the age where they will start to remember and repeat these rhymes and songs.

If you don't have a book of popular Mother Goose nursery rhymes, now would be the perfect time to purchase a book, watch videos on YouTube about these rhymes, or listen to them on iTunes. Some of the most popular books on Amazon are "Favorite Nursery Rhymes from Mother Goose" by Scott Gustafson, "Mary Engelbreit's Mother Goose: One Hundred Best-Loved Verses" by Mary Engelbreit, and "A Treasury of Mother Goose" by Hilda Offen.

Continued Growth of Language

You will start to understand what your toddler is saying, while other people might struggle. They will tell you stories and you will be able to understand most of what they say. There will be a lot of missing words as their vocabulary is over 200 words, yet they are still learning how to form these words together. Close to their third birthday, your child will understand most of what you are telling them. It's important to have as many conversations with your child and explain why something is happening. I understand the "why" question can be tiring after hearing it for the 15th time in a day, but this is one way they are learning. Take a deep breath and do your best to explain the situation calmly.

Start Explaining Your Child's Emotions

With their growth in vocabulary, you can get them to explain their emotions the best they can. They will still struggle as, let's face it, it's hard to express your emotions at times. Even adults struggle to express certain emotions. When you notice your child becoming frustrated, ask them what is making them feel this way. You want to continue asking them questions until you understand them. Then, you can start to work with them on fixing the problem. Let them try to figure it out themselves before you join in. Because they can understand you, try to give them advice or explain what they can do to solve the problem. For example, if they can't get their toy together, walk them through the process but let them put the toy together. Help them if they ask for your help or start to become more frustrated.

Nutritional Needs

By this age, your child should be nearly constantly eating three healthy meals a day and at least one snack. Of course, there will still be days where your child eats you out of house and home and days where they barely touch their food. Just like the previous year, this is normal behavior. As long as you continue to give your child options and focus on their nutrition, they will be healthy toddlers.

Meals

When it comes to meals, the biggest factor to remember is not to make it a battle. There were many times my sons didn't want to eat what was put in front of them. Yes, this is frustrating but not as frustrating as a mealtime battle will be between you and your toddler.

There are a lot of people who feel they need to pay attention to the amount of food put on their child's plate and what they eat. Don't pay attention to the amount.

You always want to eat as a family. Don't set your child's high chair away from the table or give them a child's table. While this is fine if there are more children sitting at the table, your child can start to feel separated from you. Bring them up to the table and have a mealtime conversation with them.

Don't be surprised if you plan meals and your child demands different food. The best step you can do is ensure they get the four main food groups on a daily basis.

1. Fruits and vegetables
2. Poultry, fish, eggs, and meat
3. Cereal, rice, and potatoes
4. Cheese, yogurt, milk, and other dairy products

As a warning- there will be days your child doesn't get all these food groups. This is fine as long as it doesn't happen too often. The key is to keep your child from wanting to defy you through what they eat. This can happen when you start to make mealtime a battle. They will continue the battle with nearly every meal. Take a deep breath and do what you can, such as offering them a choice or making a new recipe they may enjoy. If you are worried your child isn't getting all their nutrients, talk to their primary care physician.

Meal Plan for a day:

Breakfast: milk, egg, banana, and whole-wheat toast with jelly

Morning snack: fruit or vegetable

Lunch: milk or water, carrots, berries, and turkey on whole wheat bread or a slice of turkey cut up

Afternoon snack: cracker with cheese and water

Supper: Meat, potatoes, and a vegetable

Healthy Snacks

By this age, you will know what your toddler likes and doesn't like – at least at this time. It's important to remember that their taste buds are going to change. Therefore, foods that they don't like now, they might like in a few months or a couple of years. Keep re-introducing foods to them as you never know when they will eat the food like it's the best meal or snack in the world.

There are a variety of healthy snack ideas for your growing toddler. You can give them options for a snack, such as putting three items on a plate. Many of these healthy snack items are also great when you are on the go.

- Wheat thin crackers
- Cheese sticks
- Applesauce squeeze
- Yogurt pouches

- Leftovers
- Apple slices and other fruits
- Vegetables
- Veggie straws
- Fruit snacks (these aren't the healthiest, but we all deserve a treat now and then)
- No-bake chocolate peanut butter bars

To make the no-bake chocolate peanut butter bars you will need the following ingredients:

- Shredded unsweetened coconut
- Dark chocolate chips
- Crispy rice cereal or puffed flax cereal
- Rolled oats
- Peanut butter
- Brown rice syrup
- Vanilla
- Honey

The steps to make the bars are as follows:

1. Place parchment paper on an 8 by 8 pan. Ensure you will be able to take the bars out once they are done by pulling up the parchment paper.
2. In a large bowl, mix the dry ingredients well
3. On low heat, mix the peanut butter, chocolate chips, brown rice syrup, honey, and vanilla together until the chocolate is melted

4. Turn off the heat and add in dry ingredients. Mix well.

5. Pour mixture into the pan and allow the bars to cool and harden for at least 15 minutes.

Parenting Tips for Difficult Moments

Tantrums and Meltdowns

Because your toddler is able to understand you, it's easier to handle tantrums with verbal communication. At this age, it will become harder to distract them from a tantrum with something else. Therefore, you are going to need to adjust your tips and tricks.

The biggest factor to remember is your toddler doesn't want to make you angry or feel embarrassed. Your child faces difficult challenges daily and a temper tantrum or meltdown is their way of saying, "It's not working!" Do your best to remain calm and talk to them.

The first step is to figure out why your toddler is in the middle of a temper tantrum. This could be anything from a toy fell on their foot to they can't have the new toy they want. Your child could also start crying because they are hungry, thirsty, or tired. If it is close to naptime, bedtime, or mealtime, they are going to become frustrated easier.

Unfortunately, there is no true method to prevent temper tantrums. You just have to let them come as they happen. However, there are steps you can take to decrease the intensity of the tantrum.

- Follow your daily routine as much as possible. There will always be moments where you have a doctor's appointment, emergencies, and other events during naptime or their mealtime. You won't be able to follow the routine exactly as it's set for your child. However, do your best to follow the schedule. See if you can set the doctor appointment for a different time and run errands around your child's nap and mealtime schedule.

- If you do need to be away during meal or naptime, plan ahead. Have a balanced meal that your child can eat on the go or take time to stop at a restaurant and give your child a treat. Yes, taking your child out to a restaurant can cause you more stress or embarrassment from time to time, but that's part of being a parent. Having time with just the two of you in a special location can be a nice treat for both of you.

- Always acknowledge your child's feelings and try to get them to use their words. Get down to your child's level as this will help them feel more comfortable. For instance, your toddler starts crying in the middle of the grocery store and you aren't sure why. Kneel or bend down to your child's eye level and calmly say "Honey, tell me what's wrong. Use your words." Your child might need a few seconds to speak, but they will tell you. If your child says "I'm cold" as you are in the freezer section of the grocery store, say "I know, I am too. Let's quickly get what we need so we can get warm again."

- Take a moment to think about how many times a day you tell your toddler "no." No, they can't have that or no, they can't do that. They hear no often and most of the time there is a reason for this. No is a powerful word, but it can also be frustrating for your child to hear so often. Find other ways to say no, such as giving your child an option. If they ask to help you cut the veggies, which is dangerous for them, say, "I really need help in other ways. Would you like to stir the vegetables together or place the napkins on the table?" Your toddler loves to help at this age, so giving them options to help is going to take their mind off the more dangerous tasks.

- Do your best to avoid trigger situations. There are a lot of toys that are still too complicated for your two-year-old to understand. This is going to frustrate them, which will lead to a temper tantrum. Give them toys that are more of their level, so they will have an easier time understanding the toy.

Sleeping

By now, your child should sleep through the night pretty well. Their one naptime should not go longer than two to three hours. If you started your child on a nighttime and naptime routine around the age of one, you should continue that routine. If you haven't yet, it's time to start your child on a routine. Here are some tips to ensure your happy toddler is getting good sleep:

- Around the age of two is when you should start limiting food and drink before bedtime. It's often suggested to feed your one-year-old before bed as it helps them start to sleep through the night better. By this age, they can sleep around 11 to 12 hours without food or water. However, they will be thirsty and hungry when they wake up, so it is always good to have a breakfast plan in place. It is also helpful to leave a sippy cup of water by their bed.

- Put your child to bed when they are still awake but sleepy. At this age, your child should start or already know how to soothe themselves to sleep. When they learn to do this, they will be able to put themselves to sleep during the night.

- Don't give your child caffeine or a lot of sugar, especially a few hours before bed. They are naturally energetic and do not need to receive stimulation before bed. They need a couple of hours before their bedtime to be quiet and relaxing.

- Your two-year-old will still have nightmares, but not as much as a one-year-old. It's still helpful to have a nightlight and play soft music while they are sleeping. If they do wake up at night, they can work on soothing themselves back to sleep through the comforting music and light.

- Don't run into your child's room if they start crying. Wait a couple of minutes to see if they calm down and put themselves back to sleep. If they don't show any signs of calming down and aren't getting up, go in and check on them.

Mealtime

Here are some parental tips for your child's mealtime:

- If you haven't already started teaching your child to use table manners. They should be able to use utensils without too much trouble. They should also be able to say please and thank you. While it is not necessary to ensure your child says it at all times as this can cause an unnecessary battle, the more you use the words they more they will. You are always your toddler's role model.

- Make sure your toddler sits down to eat. This will help them understand that food is to remain in the dining room or kitchen and mealtime is a special time where the family sits down. However, if your child refuses to sit down, there is no need to make them. Your child just might not be in the mood to sit down. You can try to make them understand that sitting down is what the family does when everyone is eating, but they might not be that hungry.

- If your child starts to throw their food, ask them if they are finished. If they respond, they are not, tell them that people who are hungry don't throw food. If they continue to throw their food, take their plate away. When they start to request their food back, ask them if they are going to eat politely as you do. Once they agree to do this, give them their plate of food back.

- Your child doesn't need a large plate of food. They don't eat as much as we do. Therefore, to prevent too much waste, give them smaller portions. You can always give them second helpings if they ask for more.

- When your child is demonstrating good table manners, compliment them. You can also set up a reward system when your child is learning good manners. This might be a sticker chart that gives them certain rewards after they receive so many stickers.

Noncompliance

People struggle with noncompliance from their toddlers. We are human and will find ourselves losing our tempers with a child. You won't always be able to remain calm, no matter how hard you try. The best you can do is to do your best when it comes to dealing with difficult moments. Remind yourself that this is temporary, and your child is learning.

At two-years-old, time-out is a go-to for parents. There are always going to be parents and non-parents who have their opinions about how to discipline your child. Always remember this is your child and it is your right to decide when you will put your child in a time-out. Every child is different, which means they are going to respond to discipline differently. For instance, your friend's child might not respond to time-outs, but they respond to the loss of a toy. Your child might respond to time-outs but not losing a toy because they are happy to grab a different toy. You need to follow your child's personality when it comes to the best way to discipline.

Here are some common time-out tips:

- It's fine to give your child a time-out in public. Your two-year-old lives in the moment and is not going to remember what they did wrong at the store when you get home. Find a private spot in the store, such as a corner aisle or the public bathroom. You can even take your child out to the car and give them time to calm down. Always attend to their negative behavior immediately.

- Have a time-out spot in your home, but not in their bedroom. Placing your child in their bedroom can make them struggle when it comes to sleeping as the room won't be seen as peaceful. Have a chair in the corner of your living or kitchen or make them sit on the bottom step. Every time they go to time-out at home, they go to that spot.

- No matter what your child does, a two-year-old should only be in time-out for two minutes. Even if you believe they have done the worst action in the world, keep the time-out to two minutes.

- Have a system when it comes to giving your child a time-out. Explain to them they are going to time-out and why. Tell them they are to sit there for two minutes and when the timer goes off, you will come back to talk to them. If they get up, set them back down without saying a word. You don't need to start over again. This can drag on too long and make your child and you more frustrated.

- Once the timer goes off, go to your child and calmly ask them if they knew why they were in time out. You might have to help them explain because their vocabulary is limited, and it's been two minutes. Your child might not remember all of the behavior which caused a time-out. Making sure they explain the reason is crucial as then you know they understand.

- End the time-out with a smile or hug. You want to establish trust with your child that no matter what they do, your arms are always open for a hug. Plus, this will help your child build compassion and forgiveness.

Sleep and Napping Guidance

Establishing Routines

You have received a lot of information about how your child's sleeping routine is going to change. To give you a better idea of what to consider when establishing a routine, here are some great tips to help you establish the best routine with your child.

Main Factors to Consider as You Are Creating a Routine

- Playtime
- Wake-up time
- Bedtime
- Naptime
- Meals and snacks

When you create a routine, you want to take your child's day into consideration and not just when you want them to go to bed, wake up, and how much sleep they should get.

A Typical Day for a Two-Year-Old

This day is typical for a child with a stay-at-home parent.

1. Get your child up at around 7:30 a.m. You might find them waking up, playing in their room, or they might come out of their own. If they are still sleeping, make sure you gently wake them up.

2. Give them breakfast as soon as they wake up. This will help them continue to wake up because their metabolism will start to work.

3. Allow your child to play after breakfast. By this time, it might be around 8:30. Give your child some independent playing time, so you can do what you need to do.

4. Around 9:00 or so, sit down to play with your child. Continue to play or spend some leisure

time with them until about 10:00, when they can have their morning snack.

5. After their snack, go outside and play, even in the middle of winter. If the sun is shining and it's not dangerously cold, bundle your child up and head outside. Build a snowman or a fort. You want your child to take part in an activity, so they will be ready for their nap.

6. If your outside for an hour, bring your child in and allow them to watch a favorite cartoon or play independently as you prepare lunch.

7. Feed your child lunch around 11:45.

8. After they finish eating, give them time to calm down before their nap. While this might not always work, see if you can take a few minutes to read a book or play a quiet game. This is similar to a strategy you can use before bedtime.

9. Lay your child down around 1:00 p.m. for their nap.

10. Wake your child up from their nap by 4:00, if they don't wake up by themselves.

11. Give your child an afternoon snack and some water or juice. This is always a good time to give your child a little sugary treat, if you desire.

12. After a snack, allow your child to play with other family members or by themselves before supper.

13. After supper, allow your child to play calmly for a few minutes before you give them a bath.

14. Start their bedtime routine after their bath. They should be sleepy but still awake around 7:30 p.m., which is the perfect time for your two-year-old to fall asleep.

Your Child's Biological Clock

As you are trying to get your child set on a wake-up time, use nature's brightest light to help. About thirty minutes before your child should get up, open their shades and let the light shine. This will help set their biological clock and within a couple of weeks, they will start waking up around that time without a problem.

CHAPTER 4:

3-Year-Old to 4-Year Old

By now, you might have heard, "You think the terrible twos are bad, just wait until they are three!" This type of statement can make any parent cringe, especially as they are preparing to send their toddler off to school. But, before you become too worried about this statement, take a moment to think about how much a child grows between the age of two and three. They are learning more every day; they are becoming more independent; they are facing a lot of changes between going to school and routines at home. All this is a lot for a three-year-old to handle. At the same time, they are still struggling with explaining their emotions and knowing how to handle their frustrations and other negative feelings.

The fact is, three-year-olds aren't behaviorally worse than two-year-olds, they are just more independent and facing different challenges. As parents, we often forget to take a step back and think about what our children are going through. The more we do this, the easier it is to start to understand their outbursts and requests to be independent. After all, we are sending them to school now; a place where we don't stay with them. How can we do this and not let our children gain a little more independence?

Realistic Developmental Expectations

Riding a Tricycle or Bicycle

Now that your child has become more stable on their feet, they will become more interested in learning how to ride a tricycle or bicycle. Chances are, they have ridden in a child's car, wagon, or a smaller toddler tricycle previously. However, this is an age where you can purchase the "real deal." You can go to the store and buy a small bike with training wheels or start your child out with a tricycle. Either way, you want to find a road they can learn to ride on. It should be smooth and as clear from rocks and bumps as possible. While they will be less likely to trip with a tricycle or training wheels, if they don't feel balanced, they aren't going to want to ride. They will become scared that they will fall off or tip their bicycle if there are too many bumps, rocks, or other obstacles. Your child will naturally become a little gutsier with their riding abilities as they become comfortable with their new toy.

Language Development Grows Rapidly

Part of the reason your child's language skills blossom at this age is that they are in school and have more interaction with children their age and other adults. This doesn't mean that you didn't work with them enough while they were at home. Children often start to thrive a little more in school.

At this age, you will start to understand most of what your child is saying. While they will still struggle to pronounce some words, they will start to talk with more clarity. They will also learn how to form sentences a little more, which will help you understand them easier.

You will often catch your child struggling with their tenses. For example, they will say "I goed" instead of "I went." First, enjoy this moment and remember their cute little mix up with tenses because it's one of the moments that don't last too long. However, you also want to continue to educate your child. Therefore, you will want to correct them by stating what they said with the right tense. Don't make them feel ashamed that they didn't say it correctly. Let them know that it is okay to mix up words because it happens to everyone, which it does, even adults will mix up words from time to time.

Social Development

Your child is going to continue to thrive in social development during this age. Part of this is natural development and the other part is because of school. They will still be strong in imaginative play, which means it is a great time to make up games and focus on dress up. You might hold tea parties with your friends or find your child pretending to be a mechanic as they are taking the tires off of their cars. All of this is normal and helps them thrive socially. Let your child imagine what they want to imagine and play along with them when asked and you can.

As a parent, one of the best steps you can take during this age is to be a role model when it comes to social interactions. Make sure you get together with your friends while your children are there, so they can pay attention to how you and your friends act and talk. You might find your child mimic this behavior in front of you. If you do, it gives you the perfect opportunity to record this moment! When your child is growing and developing, it's always a good idea to have your camera ready.

Emotional Development

Your child is going to understand their emotions a little more than two-year-olds. It's also around this age that they are going to start paying more attention to how other people feel. This is the perfect age to start focusing on empathy, compassion, and asking them how they are doing. You can do this in the morning by asking your child, "How did you sleep last night?" If they say they didn't sleep well, ask them why. You can also ask your child, "How did your day go?" Even if you were with your child the whole day and you know exactly how it went, allow your child to tell you. This will help you understand your child's thought process and show your child that they should ask other people the same questions because this is what you do when you care about someone.

Nutritional Needs

When it comes to your child and eating in school, you want to ensure that you and the school are on the same page. If your child is allergic to anything, make sure you give the school everything they need so they can keep this in mind as your child goes through the lunch line or is given their snacks.

Your meal times are going to adjust for your child, just like the rest of their routine will. Fortunately, this is part of their routine that you can focus on gradually. For instance, when you wake your child up earlier, you will feed them breakfast earlier. You can also talk to your child's teacher or the school to ask when your child's class will have their snack break, when they will eat lunch, and if they get an afternoon snack. Chances are, your child is going to be hungry when they come home from school. Depending on the time they come home, as most preschools run half a day, snacks will depend on when you feed your family supper or if you give your child a snack right when they get home.

If your toddler goes to preschool in the afternoon, chances are you will feed them an early lunch, and then they will receive a snack in school. If they go to school in the morning, they will most likely receive a snack, but you will feed your child breakfast and lunch once they get home.

When your child starts school, they might start to eat food they have never tried before. If your child ever comes home to tell you that they enjoyed their lunch or snack, pay attention to what they ate as then you can incorporate this into your snack and meal plan at home. We all know how great it is to find new foods our children love to eat!

While you might feel more rushed during breakfast once school starts, it is essential that you do your best to give your child a healthy and balanced breakfast. The more well-balanced breakfast is, the better your child will be able to focus in school. Don't focus on giving them quick breakfast foods like donuts, pop tarts, or sugary cereal as they will become too energetic. While you want them to have energy in school, they will also feed off the energy from the other children. So, help your child remain in control and not become overstimulated. The more overstimulated your child is, the harder it will be for them to play with their peers and focus on learning.

Parenting Tips for Difficult Moments

Tantrums and Meltdowns

"What if my child has a temper tantrum in school?", is a thought that most parents have as they prepare their child for school. Reality is, your child's teacher is used to children throwing temper tantrums and meltdowns. They realize it is part of their job. Don't be surprised if you receive an email, call, or are requested for a meeting because of your child's behavior. None of this makes you a bad parent – it makes you a normal parent. Your child is also showing typical toddler behavior. The best you can do is handle the situation as it pops up. Your child is going to learn new behavior from other children, which is difficult to prepare for.

At this age, your child might start to decrease their temper tantrums because they can express their emotions easier. At the same time, it might also seem that your child will never stop throwing temper tantrums. Rest assured, they will stop throwing toddler temper tantrums. When it comes to a child's behavior throughout the years, they will continue to have dramatic episodes and meltdowns. But, if you think about it, adults are the same way.

Because your child is growing older, it is easier to communicate with them. As they start school, set your child down and discuss what you expect from them as they go to school and what they shouldn't do. You will need to realize that this conversation is going to happen again and again. You will sit down because of certain ways your child has acted or because of certain situations and want to explain something you didn't before. You will also need to re-explain your expectations here and there. There will be times you feel like your child isn't listening to you, but I promise, they are. Children really do forget information that we tell them because their brains are still developing.

"Is my child supposed to be throwing temper tantrums at this age? Is there something wrong?" No, there is nothing wrong with a three, almost four-year-old, throwing a temper tantrum. Yes, it is normal for children to do this, even going into five and six years old. At this age, your children shouldn't hit as often as they used to, but they still might act out in this way from time to time. As long as you continue to remain consistent when it comes to your child's actions, even once they start school, your child will learn that certain behaviors are not tolerated.

"What should I do if my child gets in trouble at school? Should I discipline them, even if they are given a time-out or detention in school?" Technically, this is completely up to you. Some parents feel if their child's teacher disciplined them, then there is nothing to worry about. Other parents do not feel this way; they feel that if their children misbehave in school, they will be in trouble at home. The biggest factor to consider is: did your child learn anything? You should always talk to your child about their behavior in school. Ask them what they learned and if they have a good response, settle the matter. If they still don't understand what they did wrong, talk to them about it.

Mealtime

"What if my child doesn't eat in school? What will they think of me as a parent? Will they let my child starve?" Three-year-old children are similar to two-year-old children when it comes to eating. Your child's teacher and other school personnel are used to children being picky eaters, eating one day and not the next, and several other factors. The school officials all understand there will be times they eat everything on their plate and there will be times where they don't eat much at all. There might even be days where they don't really touch food or snacks in school. There could be many reasons for this. If you start to worry about your child's eating behaviors, it is best to bring them to their primary care physician.

Your main focus should be meals at home. Will you need to change your child's meal routine because of school? If so, how are you going to go about doing this? You might need to put in extra work to ensure that your child gets as many well-balanced meals as possible because it is going to be easier for them to eat what they want or get snacks as they continue to grow in school. While this isn't something to stress over, it is a factor to consider, especially when your child becomes more independent.

Noncompliance

"What if my child refuses to listen to the teacher, what will I do?" Reality is, if you have taught your child manners, compassion, and talk to your child about who to listen to when they go to school, their behavior in school will amaze you. As parents, we often think about bad behaviors or stress over what other people are going to think about us as parents. Instead, we should focus on the positives. Your child is a good kid and the reason why is because of you. You are doing a great job as a parent and you deserve to tell yourself this every day. A child misbehaves from time to time, it is what they do. It's how they learn and grow. Your child is a typical child, more than you realize.

When your child starts school, you want to know the policies the school has in place for bad behavior. For example, what is the school's policy on bullying? You need to keep in mind that no matter how hard the teachers try, they can't watch every single action each child does, especially when it comes to the playground. Unfortunately, there will be times that you hear about your child getting into an altercation with another child and each child has their own story and no teachers saw what happened. When this happens, the best step to take is to listen to all sides of the story and then talk to your child privately. You will learn more about what happened through your one-on-one conversation with your child than anyone else. No matter what your child tells you, do your best to remain calm. When your child starts to notice your frustration or anger grow, they are going to become more anxious because they will think this growing frustration is because of them. This can make them double-think about what they are about to say and start to lie.

You already have routines for a time-out, so stick to these routines. They still work great for three-year-old children. At the same time, this can be an easier age to start sending them to their room for a time-out, especially when they are closer to the age of four. By now, they are comfortable in their room and sending them for a three-minute time-out in their room isn't going to disrupt their sleep.

Another step you can start to take at this age is the "think about what your actions" phase. Tell them to think about what caused them to get a time-out while they are sitting in their room or on a chair. You will be amazed by how your child actually thinks about their behavior as they are sitting in a time-out. This is because your child's mind develops continuously as a toddler and they are more aware of their actions and emotions as three-years-old. While you will still need to sit with them and discuss their behavior and help them work on better ways to control their behavior, they might start to come up with solutions themselves at the same time.

Sleep and Napping Guidance

Establishing Routines

The biggest change in their routine at this age is going to be heading to school. This might mean you need to look into changing your child's bedtime as you need to get them up earlier for school. At the same time, you will also need to adjust your child's time with you. They are used to spending most of their day with you, providing they didn't go to daycare or have a caregiver during the day. To help your child adjust to their changing routine, here are some tips.

1. Explain the change in routine ahead of time. You can do this while you are showing your child their new school or preparing them to start going to bed earlier. Explain the change as often as you feel necessary. Even when your child looks at you and says, "I know", continue to spend your time explaining the new routine and how their routine is going to continue to change. It's always going to be an anxious time for them, but they won't realize how much until they are in the moment. Your children don't think ahead as you do.

2. Focus on the positive when it comes to changes. You can do this by explaining how many friends they are going to make and how much smarter they are going to get. Remember, you are your child's role model, so you can always say, "You will grow up to be like mommy or

daddy." You can even have a little fun with this by showing your muscles or talking about how smart you are. Giving your child something to look forward to when it comes to all the changes is going to help decrease their anxiety.

3. You will need to be patient. We all lack patience from time to time, so when you feel yourself hanging on to the last thread of patience you have, take a break. You can try some deep breathing exercises, meditation, or just take a few minutes to yourself. You need to focus on self-care in order to remain patient when it comes to changing routines with your toddler. You might find yourself going back to helping them self-soothe themselves to sleep earlier. This will take you a week or two, but you will be able to accomplish it and help your child through their adjustment if you remain consistent and patient.

4. Think about their earlier wake-up time. If you can use the sun technique again, follow that. However, sometimes it is dark when your children need to wake up, especially if you are readjusting their routine during the winter months. If this happens, turn on a lamp next to their bed when they need to wake up. Do this at least 30 minutes before they need to get up, just as you would with the sun.

CHAPTER 5:

Preparing Your Child for School

Your toddler is going to go through a lot of transitions. They will make transitions at home and socially. Some of their main milestones will be when they are entering school. There are different phases of schooling, which allows your toddler to start once they enter daycare.

Daycare, Pre-School, Kindergarten

It doesn't matter which type of school your toddler is about to enter, you need to take your time to make sure they are prepared to walk through those doors. This will be a process for both you and your child, especially if you have been home with them since they were born. It is never easy leaving your child in a new location. However, it is essential for their growth and development.

You want to start looking for an early education center a few months before your child goes to school.

When it comes to an elementary school, you will often have to follow the district you live in, unless you have private schools in your location you are thinking about placing your child into. When it comes to a daycare center, you often have to get your child signed up early. Most daycare centers will fill up quickly. In order to sign up your child, you will need to contact the daycare center to see what their enrollment process is.

Preparing Your Child

Once you have chosen a school, it is important to take the time to prepare your child, so they will be comfortable with you leaving them there. It's going to take time and your child will need to adjust. They will beg you to not leave them, even weeks later. This is natural and you aren't harming their emotions or psyche by dropping them off at school. To help the process go as smoothly as possible, here are a few preparation tips:

Visit the Daycare Center or School

Always take your time to visit the location. Let your child know that they will be going to school here. Make it clear that you will not be able to stay with them, but there are a lot of wonderful people that will take good care of them. Their teachers are there to help them learn and they will make a lot of friends with the other children. You want to make it sound as exciting as possible. Your child might not act excited right away. In fact, you might notice they seem very hesitant and already start to beg you not to let them go there. While their words are going to tear at your heart, do your best to ensure they understand this is important for them.

Plan out the visit with the teacher, daycare provider, or anyone else. Try to go as a family, if possible, as this will let your child know their consistent support system is with them throughout this process. Ask them for a tour and see if your child can meet everyone. Some places will allow your child to play with the other children as you fill out paperwork or talk to the teachers. If they don't offer this opportunity, ask them if it is possible to do as this will help your child transition a little easier. Your child should be shown what their day will be like, where they will keep their backpack, where they will sit, and anything else.

Try to bring your child for a visit just a few days before they start school. If you visit a few weeks ahead of time, they are more likely to forget about the school and the people they met. This can make their transition harder.

Use Pretend Play to Help Their Transition

Your toddler's imagination runs wild and you can often use this to your advantage. Use pretend play to help your child learn what their day will be like in school. If you have a little table and chair, set them up like a desk and help your child learn. If you are able to duplicate their school schedule, do this. Otherwise, focus on playtime, learning their shapes, letters, numbers, have a snack, and read stories.

While you are playing pretend, you can start to teach your child social skills. You can explain that they will need to share, use their manners, and how to raise their hand to get their teacher's attention.

Read Books about Going to School

Another tip is to find books, such as *Llama Llama Misses Mama* by Anna Dewdney and *Maisy Goes to Preschool* by Lucy Cousins. There are a variety of books about going to school that you can easily find on Amazon or through your local library. You also want to ensure you focus on the transition itself. For example, find books that discuss how the children miss their parents but will see their parents after school is over. As you read the books, relate it to what your child is going through. Because of this, it is a great idea to continue reading books after your toddler has started school.

Change the Routine at Home Slowly

As your child starts going to school, their routine is going to change drastically, and it will happen quickly to them. This is why the adjustment is hard. Children aren't used to quick adjustments. While you can't do anything to change how quickly they will start school and how this will shift their routine, you can make the changes at home go a little slowly.

Do your best to create a peaceful and quiet environment in the home. Limit the time spent in front of the television, iPad, or any other device and focus on spending time together. Keep eating your family meals at the table and talk about your days. Your child will have a lot to say about their new school and they will be willing to talk about everything they are learning.

Going to school means your child will need to go to bed earlier to get up sooner. Prepare for this change in their schedule as this is something you can adjust for them before school starts. While we all would like the opportunity to sleep in on weekends, it's best for your child to maintain their sleeping schedule throughout the weekend and on days off. Young children in daycare and preschool should continue to have their school schedule during the summer as well. It can become too much for them to change their routine during the summer and then again in the fall.

Stay with Your Child a Few Minutes During Their First Day

Most schools will allow you to stay with your child for about 20 to 30 minutes during their first day or week. Take advantage of this and it will allow your child to adjust easier. For instance, if you are allowed to do this for the first week, gradually decrease the amount of time you stay. Play with your child and help them meet new friends for 20 minutes during the first day. Then follow your goodbye routine before you leave. Make sure you tell your child you will be back for them within a few hours. The next day, you can decrease your time to 15 minutes, 10 minutes the following day, and then five minutes. You will always bring your child in and drop them off, which means you can always spend at least five minutes with your child every morning.

Always be Involved

Even if your child has gone to an early childhood education center before going to kindergarten, it is still going to be an adjustment. Do whatever you can to work your child through the adjustment. While some students in their classroom will remain the same, the teachers will change. This can cause your child to feel stressed as they were comfortable with their previous teacher and don't understand why they need to have a new teacher. Try to get them to understand why and meet their new teacher before school starts. Fortunately, most schools have a back to school night where your child gets to see their classroom, get organized, and meet their teachers. Take advantage of this time and make sure you bring your child.

Strategies and Tips to Prepare Your Child for Peer Interaction

Oh, the friends they will meet when they start school. They will become friends with their peers, there will be fights, they will make up, and their friends will move. They will also start competing with each other, whether this is in an intellectual or physical way. Of course, this type of competing will focus more on older toddlers than the younger ones.

There is a lot that comes with preparing your child for peer interaction and ensuring that everything runs as smoothly as possible. Of course, there is going to be drama and difficult moments. However, you will all get through them as long as you continue to support your child.

Communication

Fortunately, you have been communicating with your toddler since they were born, so they know that people should talk to each other. However, they don't understand the importance of communication. This is something that they aren't going to understand as toddlers completely. But you may want to make sure they understand that everyone should get a chance to talk.

Around the age of two, you can teach your child to retain eye contact as they are talking. Your toddler is naturally going to try to avoid eye contact by looking at their toy as they talk or around the room because it helps them stay in control of their situation. When it comes to communication, giving other people your full attention to eye contact is important. One way to teach your child to maintain eye contact is through greeting people. Practice meeting your child through pretend play. You can each change your names and pretend you are different people each time you meet each other. Always praise your child when you notice they maintain eye contact as they are talking.

Other communication skills your child should know by the age of four is how to say sorry, please, and thank you. This is something that you can easily prepare your child before or during school. Fortunately, most teachers will also help your child remember their manners.

Group Play and Work

It's always a good idea to establish play dates when your child is young, especially if they are an only child. This will help ease them into playing with peers once they start school. Learning to play with other children will help them realize the importance of working with other children. At the same time, it is essential that you understand children under the age of three to four are going to play by themselves more than with other children.

When your child first starts playing with other children, it might seem that they are off in their own little world. In a way, they kind of are, as they are playing by themselves more than with the other children. This doesn't mean that they are shy, it simply means they are trying to get a feel of their surroundings. Toddlers always need to trust their surroundings and people around them before they will play without a care in the world. Let your child work get a feel and understand their environment. This is something they need to do on their own.

Once your child is in school, they will start to learn other group play and work skills. In fact, they will build on these skills in their early elementary years. Because of this, you don't need to make sure that your child knows absolutely everything possible when it comes to group work. You want to focus on teaching them skills such as patience, taking turns, and helping their peers. Once they gain the foundations of group play, they will continue to grow into children comfortable working in a group setting.

Teach Your Child Non-Verbal Cues

Many parents don't realize the importance of teaching their children how to read non-verbal cues. But this is something that is highly important when it comes to playing and working with their peers. One of the best ways to help your child learn to read non-verbal cues is to let them watch a tv show but turn the sound off. This will get them to focus on facial expressions and gestures to know what is going on instead of listening to the words.

You can also help your child learn non-verbal cues by being open and honest with them. Doing this will force you to become aware of your facial expressions and gestures. For instance, if your child tells you something that causes you to smile, you can tell them you are smiling because you are happy.

As your child grows up, they will continue to learn non-verbal cues, and you will find them asking people why they are sad or mad. Similar to group play, you won't be able to teach your child everything there is to know about non-verbal cues. However, you will be able to help them start learning.

Express Emotions

Because I discussed teaching your child to express their emotions earlier, I am not going to focus heavily on this here. I wanted you to know that this is one step to preparing your child for school. Because you have already been working on getting them to express their emotions, especially when they throw a temper tantrum or have a meltdown, you are well on your way to prepare them for school. This is an important point to make. Everything that you are trying to teach your child from the moment you bring them home will help them become ready for school and life. You help them get ready for school by teaching them how to feed themselves, reading to them, getting them to learn their shapes and colors. Don't feel that you are now at the point where you need to quickly prepare your child for school and start wishing you would have done this sooner because you've already been working on it.

Compassion

Compassion is something that sometimes falls to the side as we are trying to help our children develop their minds. With this said, it is important to realize that one of the foundations of working with peers is compassion. You are the best example when it comes to teaching your child compassion because you are their role model. It doesn't matter if you are talking directly to your child or on the phone with a friend. If your child can hear you talking, they are going to pay attention to what you are saying. You might think they are quietly playing in their own little world and not paying attention to anyone in their environment, but you are wrong. Toddlers are always alert to what is going on in their environment.

It's important to remember that children are naturally selfish, especially at a young age. They can go through the "mine" stage and constantly talk about themselves and show kindness at the same time. Compassion is going to grow with your toddler. For instance, a four-year-old is going to show more compassion than a two-year-old just because of development.

CHAPTER 6:

Teaching Your Child to Problem Solve and be More Independent

There were so many times I have wanted to fix all my sons' problems. But I knew that I couldn't because instead of helping them, I would simply be holding them back. I want them to depend on me, come to me, and ask me anything. This is one of the biggest reasons I, like you, want to jump up and do absolutely everything I can for my children. I also know, as you do, how this can keep them from going out in the world with confidence and learning from their mistakes. After all, making mistakes is one of the biggest ways we learn, grow, solve problems, and become more independent.

I understand when you struggle to take a step back and watch your child try to figure out a new toy. I understand how hard this is because it pains us emotionally to see our children struggle. However, I also know the thrill you and your child feel when they are able to overcome an obstacle. We often have tears in our eyes as we tell our child "Good job! I am so proud of you!" I know I teared up when I've watched my children succeed. It's what we dream about as parents, even the little successes.

Tips on Teaching Your Children How to Problem-Solve

In order to do our best for our children, we often focus on the various tips we receive from other parents. Therefore, I am going to share tips with you about how you can help your child learn problem-solving skills at any age.

Give Your Child an Obstacle

Giving your child a roadblock sounds like the opposite of what you want to do. However, think of it this way – if you are able to place an obstacle in front of your child, you can do so strategically. This means you are able to think about your child's problem-solving skills and make sure there is a solution for them that they can figure out. This will help them build their confidence when it comes to solving problems and allow you to see them thrive.

Don't Hover Over Your Child

I know we all want to do this. It's hard to see our babies grow up – actually, we always consider them our baby. But if you want the help your child succeed you will know when you need to back away and let them take care of the situation themselves. For instance, your child comes home from school and tells you that another child pushed them. You look at your child and, while you want to go to your child's defense, you take a deep breath and asked them what they did. Your child responds, "I told them that isn't nice and not to do that again or I will tell." At this point, you still might want to hover over your child and go to school the next day to inform the teacher what happened; but you know it's more important not to at this time. Instead, you focus on praising your child because you are proud of how they handled themselves. This tells your child that you care about what happens to them, but they are also able to take care of themselves. It also gives them the confidence to know how to handle people who are mean to them in a compassionate and polite way.

Another way we can find ourselves hovering over our children is by not giving them enough space. This not only includes independent playtime, but space to make mistakes, figure out what happened, and learn from them. Toddlers will need a little guidance when it comes to figuring out their mistakes and learning how to change their behavior or actions, so the mistake doesn't pop up again. Helping your child in this way is not hovering. You start to hover when you stop your child from making a mistake.

Make Problem-Solving a Positive Experience

Everyone runs into problems on a daily basis. We all have problems we need to solve. We might not always see them as problems, but they are there. Take time to reflect on your days and notice what problems occur in your life. Then, think of your toddler's days and their struggles. Figure out ways that you can turn everyone's problem-solving experience into a more fun and positive situation. For instance, if your child comes to you with a problem, look at them and say "I see what your problem is. Why don't we think of a couple of solutions together to help solve this problem?" With your toddlers, you can also make this into a game. For example, if they like Sherlock Holmes, they can play Sherlock and you can be Watson trying to solve a problem.

Do-It-Yourself Projects

There are tons of do-it-yourself type projects for people of all ages. While your child can help you with home improvement projects at times, there are also smaller projects that you can work on with your child. You don't need to make sure that you do everything correctly or don't ask for help. Your child is going to learn more about solving their own problems by watching you solve yours. Therefore, if they see you ask for help, they will understand that everyone asks for help. If your child sees you make a mistake, they will know that they can make a mistake, and everything will be okay.

Along with these types of projects, you can also look into puzzles. By the age of four, your child has probably put together tons of puzzles, which is a way that helps them problem solve. Continue to buy your child puzzles, but make sure that they are age-appropriate.

Problem Solving By Ages

One-Year-Old Problem-Solving Skills

While one-year-olds who are closer to two might start helping you put puzzles together or shapes in the correct spot, most of their skills are going to happen through observation. Have you ever stopped to think about how often a one-year-old will sit and watch other people? This is because the main way they learn and start to develop their skills is through observing, listening, and taking in what is going on around them. At the same time, their mind is busy processing all the information they are taking in.

One of the best ways to help your one-year-old develop problem-solving skills is by showing them how to do something. For example, your child received new stackable blocks from your sibling. At first, they look at the blocks and seem puzzled. They might pick up a block and observe it more closely. At that moment, they don't understand that the blocks are meant to be stacked on top of each other. Therefore, you will take the time to show your child how the blocks work. Once you do this, hand the blocks over to your child and watch them mimic your actions. It's always an adventure to see how your young child catches on to what you have shown them so quickly!

Problem-Solving Activities

- Play a variety of easy games for one-year-old children that will build their problem-solving skills, such as blocks and puzzles

- Playing peek-a-boo.
- Use objects to play hide-and-seek. You want your child to find the object. At this age, they are learning that just because they can't see an object, doesn't mean it doesn't exist.

Two-Year-Old Problem-Solving Skills

At two-years-old, memory comes onto the stage and gives your child a whole new way to learn how to problem-solve. This is a great age to start to bring easy puzzles and games which will help build your child's problem-solving skills. Just like a one-year-old, the biggest ways two-year-olds are going to learn is through observing. The only difference is, they are going to remember what they saw for a longer time.

Your child wants to color. They have asked you to help them get their crayons, but you are in the middle of preparing supper, which means that your hands are greasy and full of food you don't wish to get on the drawer where the crayons stay. You tell your toddler, "Go ahead and open the drawer, you can do it." At first, they look at you, at the drawer, and look at you again. They have never opened the drawer before, so they are a bit anxious about being able to get it open. You assure them that they will be able to open the drawer just fine. "Open the drawer like I do," you tell your child. They then walk to the drawer as you start to wash your hands. You know that they have only been able to shake and bang the drawer in hopes of opening it. They have never opened it before, so you are preparing to help your child. However, your child surprises you, and perhaps themselves, as they pull the handle and open the drawer without too much of struggle. "Look at what you did, baby!" You exclaim as you clap with your child's excitement.

At two-years-old, your child will use their memory to think about ways to solve a problem. They will start to come up with solutions in their mind and then see if this solution works. This is often why two-year-old children will stare at the problem before they try anything. It's not because they are becoming frustrated or thinking about giving up. They are trying to figure out how the toy works. The best step you can take is to observe your child. Notice their facial expressions as they are thinking and get an understanding of their thought process. You will also want to observe them so you can ask them if they would like to help if they become frustrated.

Problem-Solving Activities:

- Teach your child how to play "Simon Says"
- Use words like "over," "under," and "above" as this will help your child figure out what these words mean. They are great words to use when your child is looking for a toy that might be under the table.
- Gets toys and puzzles that let your child sort pieces through shapes and colors.

Three-Year-Old Problem-Solving Skills

Three-year-old children will often show a look of focus, yet they will become frustrated. They will use memory to solve problems but are more prone to trial and error than a two-year-old child. This is because three-year-old children are going to try things their way more than through observation or with help from their parents. This is also one reason why many people say that threes are worse than twos. It's because your three-year-old toddler is going to try a variety of new and interesting problem-solving skills while you are in another room. You won't have a clue what they are getting themselves into until you walk into the room for the surprise.

By now, your child has learned about the wonders of tape and glue. They have learned that if they want to put something together, they can use one of these supplies to do so. Your child is an artist and they have torn up little pieces of colored paper that they want to display on a larger sheet of paper. As they start to place the torn-up pieces of paper, your child notices they won't stay where they set the pieces. Instead of becoming frustrated, your toddler thinks back to how they saw you tape pieces of paper together before. They then find the tape (even if it is up in a cupboard, they know how to move chairs) and start to tape the little pieces onto the big piece.

This is when a new problem arises as the tape gets stuck in places, they did not want the tape to go. This starts to frustrate your toddler, but they are determined to figure it out. Their independence has reached a whole new level, which is why they often keep from asking for help. Thinking back to all the times they have seen you or someone else use tape, they realize that their pieces of tape are a lot bigger than your pieces. They then try to focus on getting smaller pieces of tape. Unfortunately, this becomes a problem as well because it's not always easy to get small pieces of tape. By this point, most three-year-old children will become frustrated, but they are also very determined little people. It might take them several trial and error moments, but they will problem-solve and complete the task.

Problem-Solving Activities

- Puzzles that are age-appropriate are going to make your child think about solutions.
- Allow your child to come up with solutions to their own obstacles. Even if they are making a mess, let them make mistakes and learn.

Chapter 7:

Additional Resources

Your child is going to continue to grow, which means that there is a lot more material you will need to help ensure you are doing the best for your child. I know how it is – we want to read all the books we can and check out all the websites we feel are available to us. While we can never read everything possible on raising children, we can do our best to get the best sense of what is out there. This is one reason I wanted to spend time giving you further resources to help as your child continues to grow and develop. All of the books are available on Amazon, which is always a plus for busy parents. There are also several materials that are available online.

Language Development

My Toddler Talks: Strategies and Activities to Promote Your Child's Language Development by Kimberly Scanlon.

My Toddler Talks is a great book for parents who are concerned that their children aren't talking as much as they should. It will help you feel at ease and provide you with plenty of resources and strategies to help increase your child's vocabulary. Through the activities and strategies, Scanlon explains how you can help your toddler thrive by giving a scientific approach from her background as a speech-language pathologist.

Scanlon's book includes a variety of topics, such as straightforward instructions and step by step directions on how to get your child to communicate, a system that will help you track your child's growing vocabulary. There are also charts which will allow you to monitor your child's progress. But, the fun of this book does not stop here. You will also receive 25 play routines that are created specifically to help your child talk more and advice for when your child runs into obstacles (Scanlon, 2012).

PBS KIDS 100 Phrases for Toddlers: First Words and Phrases for 2-3 Year-Olds by The Early Childhood Experts at PBS Kids.

This is a great book brought to you by experts who work at PBS. As parents, we struggle to understand our children from time to time. We also struggle when it comes to explaining certain things to our two-year-old because they can't understand everything we understand. It's hard to know exactly what they can understand from our conversations and what they can't. If you want to learn more about your toddler's vocabulary, this is a book to look into.

How does this book help you understand your child's language skills? It works by helping you build your child's vocabulary through the book. The experts who wrote this book spent years looking at research to see what words and phrases two-year-old children tend to use. They then put this information into a book. Furthermore, this book will help push your child into problem-solving by thinking about the shapes, colors, and images within the pages of the book. (PBS KIDS 100 Phrases for Toddlers: First Words and Phrases for 2-3 Year-Olds, 2017).

Small Talk: How to Develop Your Child's Language Skills from Birth to Age Four by Nicola Lathey and Tracey Blake.

Small Talk is a very thorough book going from birth until the age of four. In this book, you will learn about your child's limited vocabulary at every age. You will also learn the reason behind the babbling stage and why it is important to ensure your babies are talking away in their own language. This book also discusses how even though we can't understand what our baby is saying, it is important that we respond and carry on a conversation with our child. This can help your child start to develop their vocabulary, especially when we remember to use smaller words.

Small Talk also gives you advice on how to communicate with your child when they are throwing a temper tantrum. This is something that every parent should know because every child is going to have dozens of tantrums throughout their toddler years. As I discussed earlier, it is hard to communicate with your child because of their limited vocabulary. Therefore, the more strategies and techniques you can try when your child is developing the language, the better your communication (Lathey & Blake, 2014).

What About Websites?

When it comes to online websites, there are many sources available for language development. Some of the best sources to check out are medical websites, such as Mayo Clinic and the Cleveland Clinic. These websites will not only explain where your child should sit with language at a certain age but will also make you aware of signs to look for when it comes to development delays.

It is important to note that no parent wants to hear their child is delayed in development. At the same time, this is nothing to worry about. First, it is important to remember that you have to be aware your child is going to go at their own pace. They might not want to talk because they are shy, or they are growing into a naturally quiet person. Just because your two-year-old only says a few words when you ask them a question or is more prone to using sign language doesn't mean they won't find their voice within a few years.

Other websites to check out online are educational websites. There are a lot of colleges that like to share their studies about language development in toddlers. Furthermore, there are professors and other professionals who enjoy writing articles about their profession in order to help other parents.

Potty Training

Potty Training in 3 Days: The Step-by-Step Plan for a Clean Break from Dirty Diapers by Brandi Brucks.

Potty Training in 3 Days is a book that is going to catch the attention of almost every parent. We all have busy lives, which means we all want to find ways to complete certain tasks as quickly as possible. For many parents, this includes potty training. Not only does this book give you advice on how to potty train your child within three days, but it also helps you learn strategies to help you remain calm. At the same time, you will be able to learn what is going on in your child's mind. What are they thinking about potty training and how scary is the potty to them? You will be able to gain answers to questions, such as, "Should I start my child out on a toddler potty?" (Brucks, 2016).

It Hurts When I Poop! a Story for Children Who Are Scared to Use the Potty by Howard J. Bennett

One of the best ways to help your child through the transition from diapers to using the potty is by reading books that show them it's okay to use the potty. Your child is going to be scared of using the potty because it is different for them. Plus, to a toddler, the toilet can be a pretty big thing that they cannot figure out how it actually works. Remember, toddlers figure out everything by learning how they work. While they can see everything go down when they flush the toilet, they are not going to understand where everything goes. On top of this, many children can be afraid to sit on the toilet because it's rather big while they are small. They can, and they do, easily fall in. While this is more likely to give them a scare than harm them, it's always best to start them on a toddler's potty and then move them onto the toilet with a toddler's toilet seat attachment.

Oh Crap! Potty Training: Everything Modern Parents Need to Know to Do It Once and Do It Right by Jamie Glowacki.

When we are taking on a new adventure with our children, we want to learn everything we can about the situation. This is why Glowacki's book is helpful for parents who are new to the whole potty training experience. In this book, the author shares her own six-step guide to successfully potty training your toddler. You will also learn how to tell your child is ready. Like most situations in your toddler's world, they need to be ready in order to take part in the action. If they are not ready, it's most likely not going to work or happen. Therefore, in order to make sure that potty training is successful, you have to ensure your child is ready. Other factors this book discusses is how to get your daycare provider in agreement with your potty training plan and why your child is going to regress when they have done so well.

What's on the Internet?

Just like with language development, you can read medical articles which will allow you to get a good idea about potty training. At the same time, this is one of the most popular topics when it comes to your child. Because of this, there are dozens of helpful websites from blog posts written by parents who have successfully potty trained their child to sites which discuss some of the most popular books. If you are brand new to potty training, doing a quick Google search can help you get an idea of where your child's road is about to head. You can not only learn various strategies and tips to help your child get through potty training, but you can also read about other parents' mistakes when it comes to potty training.

Traveling with Toddlers

I can't tell you how many parents I have talked to who discuss not wanting to travel because they have toddlers. While I understand this completely, I also want to inform you that you shouldn't let any worry about how your child is going to react while traveling to keep you and your family from making memories and seeing the world. Sure, your toddler isn't going to remember everything as they are a bit too young. However, they will still have one of the best experiences.

Traveling With Toddlers: Information and Activities for a Happy Holiday by Gayle Jervis and Kristen Jervis Cacka.

The best way to start preparing for traveling with your toddler is to learn everything you can for yourself. "Traveling with Toddlers" is a great book to start with as this gives you some of the best information you need to know. The main concept of this book is to minimize stress as much as possible. In order to do this, you learn how to prepare your toddler for the trip. You also learn about your toddler's routine. How is traveling going to affect their routine? Can and should you create a whole new routine as you travel? How is your child going to react to traveling? On top of this, you will receive tips on how to pack your child's suitcase, how to pack the car, and several other tips and tricks to get you through traveling so you and your family can have a happy vacation.

Maisy Goes on a Plane: A Maisy First Experiences Book by Lucy Cousins

Maisy is a popular series of books for toddlers. Like the "Llama Llama" series, Maisy goes through situations that your toddler is going to go through. By reading books as you discuss what is going to happen with your toddler, you can give them a sense of calm. While they will still be anxious and have meltdowns on the trip, they will be a little more at ease because the characters they love, such as Maisy, went on trips and everything was okay and fun.

Amazing Airplanes (Amazing Machines) by Tony Mitton and Ant Parker

Because your toddler becomes comfortable with new situations by learning how they work, you can always find books like *Amazing Airplanes* which will show your toddler how airplanes work. You can also try YouTube to see what type of fun and interesting videos you can find for your toddler. However, if you are unable to find cartoon-type videos, you might have a hard time getting your toddler interested.

What's on the Internet?

When it comes to websites, you will find a lot of tips and strategies from parents who have traveled with their toddler. They will discuss what worked and what didn't. They will also give you other advice, such as factors they wish they would have thought of or known before they decided to take a vacation with their child. You will also get information about what you should pack for your toddler. Your child is known to go through a lot of clothes, so how many outfits and shoes should you pack for a trip? How many toys are you going to need to take with you, so your child doesn't become bored? How do you know if you are packing too much? All of your questions can easily be answered through the materials we discussed.

Conclusion

Raising toddlers is not an easy task. Raising your children is going to be the hardest job you have ever had. Yet, it is also going to be the most rewarding and will give you more amazing experiences and memories than you could ever imagine. You live for your children in many ways; most parents do. We are extremely prideful when it comes to our children, and these are amazing factors to have as parents.

At the same time, we want to do whatever we can to ensure our toddlers have the best life possible. While this is a great goal to have in mind, we often forget that it means we need to step back and let them make their own mistakes and decisions. Toddlers are learning so much in a fast-paced way. This can cause them to become stressed and overloaded very easily. What we find as simple tasks, they are going to have to think about and problem-solve before they can come up with a solution. We can often lose patience when this happens because we feel rushed in our lives. It's important to do our best to remember to take a few steps back and realize that the process our child is going through is more important than making sure we get to the grocery store at a certain time. In fact, if you need to stay home a couple of minutes longer and be a bit late for your doctor's appointment because you needed to take care of your child's temper tantrum, this is exactly what you do.

I created this book because I wanted to help you. As a parent of two boys myself, I understand what you are going through. I know the emotions you face as you hear your child start screaming at the top of their lungs in public. I know the struggles you face when it comes to trying to understand what your one-year-old is saying. I understand how you question yourself and wonder if you are making the best decisions for your child. Like you, I have felt alone and at my wits end when it comes to parenting. I have felt like there was nowhere left to turn and I either needed a break or I was going to lose it. Trust me, you are not alone. There are other parents who have those same creeping thoughts of "if I could only get a few minutes of peace" followed by guilt because this means you want to be away from your toddler for a short period of time. There is no reason you should feel this guilt. After all, you need to take care of yourself, so you can provide the best life for your toddler.

Through the developmental expectations described in this book, you have a better understanding of the behaviors of your child and what behaviors they will grow into. It's important to remember that the steps your child is taking in their development are the same steps other children take. Your child is doing their best to understand the world around them – a world that we have grown up with for years. Because of this, we need to do what we can to remain calm and have patience for our toddlers who are always in amazement of what the world has to offer.

Finally, your child is in the best hands because you are their best provider and teacher. By understanding your toddler the best you can, you will help them thrive in their development. They will gain mastery skills because you gave them your love, attention, and effort. This is something that no one else can give them. Be as proud of yourself as you are watching your toddler grow into an independent, compassionate, and amazing person.

References

10 Ways to Teach your Children to be Problem Solvers | All Pro Dad. Retrieved 22 August 2019, from https://www.allprodad.com/10-ways-to-teach-your-children-to-be-problem-solvers/

18 Month Old Sleep Schedule. (2017). Retrieved 20 August 2019, from https://www.nanit.com/blog/baby-sleep-schedule/18-month-baby-sleep-schedule/

An Easy Peasy 2-Year-Old Routine That Works Every Time. Retrieved 22 August 2019, from https://amotherfarfromhome.com/2-year-old-sample-routine/

Barney - Clean Up Lyrics. Retrieved 20 August 2019, from http://www.metrolyrics.com/clean-up-lyrics-barney.html

Beaudry, C. Toddler Milestones: 18-24 Months. Retrieved 21 August 2019, from https://www.parents.com/toddlers-preschoolers/development/growth/milestones-18-24-months/

Child Development and Early Learning: A Foundation for Professional Knowledge and Competencies. Retrieved 22 August 2019, from https://www.nap.edu/resource/19401/ProfKnowComp FINAL.pdf

Diproperzio, L. (2011). The Year Ahead: Age 3. Retrieved 22 August 2019, from https://www.parents.com/toddlers-preschoolers/development/growth/developmental-milestones-age-three/

Feeding & Nutrition Tips: Your 2-Year-Old. (2017). Retrieved 21 August 2019, from https://www.healthychildren.org/English/ages-stages/toddler/nutrition/Pages/Feeding-and-Nutrition-Your-Two-Year-Old.aspx

Fruit & Yogurt Baby Smoothie. Retrieved 21 August 2019, from https://www.happyfamilyorganics.com/learning-center/recipes-meal-plans/fruity-yogurt-smoothie/

Fruit & Yogurt Popsicle Recipe. Retrieved 20 August 2019, from https://www.happyfamilyorganics.com/learning-center/recipes-meal-plans/fruit-yogurt-pops/

Gavin, M. (2014). Toddlers at the Table: Avoiding Power Struggles (for Parents). Retrieved 21 August 2019, from https://kidshealth.org/en/parents/toddler-meals.html

Gottesman, N. Dining Dramas: Toddler Feeding Problems, Solved. Retrieved 20 August 2019, from https://www.parents.com/toddlers-preschoolers/feeding/problems/toddler-feeding-problems-solved/

How to Prepare Your Child for Preschool. Retrieved 21 August 2019, from https://www.brighthorizons.com/family-resources/how-to-prepare-your-child-for-preschool

Leaver, L. (2004). Overcoming Sleep Struggles. Retrieved 20 August 2019, from https://www.parents.com/toddlers-preschoolers/sleep/issues/overcoming-sleep-struggles/

Lovecraft, T. (2018). 6 Vital Social Skills to Teach to Preschool Children. Retrieved 22 August 2019, from https://www.emergingedtech.com/2018/08/vital-social-skills-to-teach-pre-school-children/

Lullaby lyrics: Itsy-Bitsy Spider. (2018). Retrieved 22 August 2019, from https://www.babycenter.com/0_lullaby-lyrics-itsy-bitsy-spider_6729.bc

Morin, A. Developmental Milestones for 2-Year-Olds. Retrieved 21 August 2019, from https://www.understood.org/en/learning-attention-issues/signs-symptoms/developmental-milestones/developmental-milestones-for-typical-2-year-olds

My Toddler Talks: Strategies and Activities to Promote Your Child's Language Development. (2012). Retrieved 23 August 2019, from https://www.amazon.com/Toddler-Talks-Strategies-Activities-Development-ebook/dp/B00AAZO27W/ref=sr_1_1?keywords=Language+development+for+toddlers&qid=1566537166&s=gateway&sr=8-1

Palanjian, A. (2019). No-Bake Chocolate Peanut Butter Bars: So Easy & Healthy. Retrieved 22 August 2019, from https://www.yummytoddlerfood.com/recipes/desserts/no-bake-chocolate-peanut-butter-bars/

PBS KIDS 100 Phrases for Toddlers: First Words and Phrases for 2-3 Year-Olds. (2017). Retrieved 23 August 2019, from https://www.amazon.com/PBS-KIDS-100-Phrases-Toddlers/dp/1941367364/ref=sr_1_4?keywords=Language+development+toddlers&qid=1566538335&s=gateway&sr=8-4

Potty Training in 3 Days: The Step-by-Step Plan for a Clean Break from Dirty Diapers. (2016). Retrieved 23 August 2019, from https://www.amazon.com/Potty-Training-Days-Step-Step-ebook/dp/B01M2WR88O/ref=sr_1_16?keywords=Language+development+for+toddlers&qid=1566537860&s=gateway&sr=8-16

PublicDomainPictures. (2012). Free Image on Pixabay - Baby, Child, Cute, Doll, Expression. Retrieved 19 August 2019, from https://pixabay.com/photos/baby-child-cute-doll-expression-17366/

Small Talk: How to Develop Your Child's Language Skills from Birth to Age Four. (2014). Retrieved 23 August 2019, from https://www.amazon.com/Small-Talk-Develop-Childs-Language-ebook/dp/B00K00AIQQ/ref=sr_1_3?keywords=toddlers+develop+language&qid=1566539084&s=gateway&sr=8-3

Spinach Mini-Muffins for Toddlers. Retrieved 20 August 2019, from https://www.happyfamilyorganics.com/learning-center/recipes-meal-plans/super-green-mini-muffins/

StockSnap. (2017). Free Image on Pixabay - Kid, Child, Boy, Mopping, Jeans. Retrieved 20 August 2019, from https://pixabay.com/photos/kid-child-boy-mopping-jeans-2586010/

Temper Tantrum – How To Deal With Toddler Tantrums (7 Proven Steps). (2019). Retrieved 21 August 2019, from https://www.parentingforbrain.com/deal-toddler-temper-tantrums/

Temper tantrums in toddlers: How to keep the peace. (2018). Retrieved 21 August 2019, from https://www.mayoclinic.org/healthy-lifestyle/infant-and-toddler-health/in-depth/tantrum/art-20047845

thedanw. (2015). Free Image on Pixabay - Music, Kids, Children, Play. Retrieved 19 August 2019, from https://pixabay.com/photos/music-kids-children-play-xylophone-818459/

Toddlers and mealtime manners. Retrieved 22 August 2019, from https://www.betterhealth.vic.gov.au/health/HealthyLiving/toddlers-and-mealtime-manners

Toddlers Pictures | Download Free Images on Unsplash. Retrieved 22 August 2019, from https://unsplash.com/search/photos/toddlers

Traumland-de. (2014). Free Image on Pixabay - Baby, Mirror Image, Mirror. Retrieved 20 August 2019, from https://pixabay.com/photos/baby-mirror-image-mirror-mirrored-536412/

What to expect for physical development between 12 and 18 months. (2013). Retrieved 18 August 2019, from https://www.healthyfamiliesbc.ca/home/articles/physical-development-toddlers-12-18-months

What you need to know about toddler cognitive development at 12-18 Months | Healthy Families BC. (2013). Retrieved 18 August 2019, from https://www.healthyfamiliesbc.ca/home/articles/toddlers-cognitive-development-12-18-months